I0165856

Neighbours who share a common postcode are unlikely to share a common mindset or worldview. This plurality is the multiverse that Martin Davie introduces and summarises so that Christians can be better equipped to understand, engage and witness to their neighbours.

Ed Moll, Vicar of St George's Church, Wembdon and Trustee of the Latimer Trust.

Martin Davie has a broad sweep of understanding of the world in which we live, and the Christian critique of its philosophical frameworks. Drawing on Christian history and biblical theology, he has summarised for anyone wanting to survey the current scene a view of the major narratives that compete for adherents today. This will be a helpful overview and stimulus to explore further, especially for young Christians trying to engage with the multiple varied beliefs of their friends and colleagues.

Paul Perkin, Vicar of St Andrew's Church, Limpsfield Chart.

It is amazing how much Martin Davie can pack into a short space. In this short book he has given a succinct summary of ten current worldviews, secular and religious, that form the core beliefs of millions of fellow citizens. The term multiverse is not intended in this instance to mean the speculations about possible parallel universes, but to engage with the creeds of non-religious believers and the followers of seven of the world's most well-known religions. Given the word-limit of a short manifesto that compares the Christian faith with each of the other systems of belief, he has produced a brief, but fair, description in each case, attentive to how each presents itself.

The main purpose of the study is to provide a guide for Christians, living in a thoroughly pluralist society, as to how they should 'live well' in the multiverses that surround them. He proposes three key activities: understanding the beliefs of others, standing firm in their own convictions, and reaching out to share God's story with friends, colleagues, neighbours and, where appropriate, their own families. This provides an excellent concise presentation of key specific points that will help Christians to engage with other people's multiverse and commend their own.

Andrew Kirk, Trustee and Research Fellow for the Kirby Laing Centre for Public Theology.

Living in a Multiverse

A Guide for Christians

Martin Davie

The Latimer Trust

Living in a Multiverse: A Guide for Christians © Martin Davie 2024. All rights reserved.
ISBN 978-1-916834-05-7 Published by the Latimer Trust May 2024.

The Latimer Trust (formerly Latimer House, Oxford) is a conservative Evangelical research organisation within the Church of England, whose main aim is to promote the history and theology of Anglicanism as understood by those in the Reformed tradition. Interested readers are welcome to consult its website for further details of its many activities.

The Latimer Trust
London N14 4PS UK
Registered Charity: 1084337
Company Number: 4104465
www.latimertrust.org
administrator@latimertrust.org

Views expressed in works published by The Latimer Trust are those of the authors and do not necessarily represent the official position of The Latimer Trust.

Contents

Introduction: Welcome to the Multiverse

Why we live in a multiverse

C S Lewis' Narnia stories are well known. However, one feature of these stories that is generally overlooked is the fact that they are set in a multiverse – in other words, a world in which there are multiple parallel universes. In the Narnia stories, Lewis' characters move between our universe and the universe in which Narnia exists. In *The Magician's Nephew*, it is made clear that our universe and the Narnian universe are just two among multiple universes which exist alongside each other.[1]

Lewis is by no means the only fiction writer to explore the idea of the multiverse. Numerous other writers have done so as well, and it is an idea that has also been explored in films and television series. For example, the three, linked Warner Brothers television series – *The Flash*, *Supergirl* and *Arrow* – are set in a multiverse with characters and story lines moving between different universes.

What is more, the idea that there might be multiple universes existing alongside each other is one that has been proposed not just by the creators of fiction, but by serious scientists as well. For example, the late Stephen Hawking in his book, *The Grand Design*, posits the existence of multiple universes each with

---

1 C. S. Lewis, *The Magician's Nephew* (London: Harper Collins, 2009), Ch.3.

their own physical laws.[2] The idea is also put forward by Laura Mersini-Houghton in her recent book *Before the Big Bang: The Origin of Our Universe from the Multiverse*.[3]

However, there is no consensus among scientists about the validity of the multiverse idea – and, at the moment, there seems to be no hard evidence to support it. In the words of the theoretical physicist John Polkinghorne, 'There is no purely scientific reason to believe in an ensemble of universes.'[4] However, there is another way of looking at the multiverse idea. Not only are there multiple universes, but people in the UK are inhabiting them.

In his helpful book, *The Universe Next Door*, James Sire draws attention to the fact that, whether they know it or not, everyone has a worldview, a way of understanding the world in which they live and their place in it.[5] These different worldviews means that people living in the same street may well live in radically different conceptual universes. For instance, Angela may live in a universe which is governed by a creator God who has acted to save the world through Jesus Christ, and in which she will be resurrected by God at the end of time. Meanwhile, her neighbour Charles lives in a universe without God, in which everything is controlled by the random interaction of

2 Stephen Hawking, *The Grand Design* (London: Bantam, 2010).
3 Laura Mersini-Houghton, *Before the Big Bang: The Origin of Our Universe from the Multiverse* (London: Bodley Head, 2022).
4 John Polkinghorne, *One World* (London: SPCK, 1986), 80.
5 James Sire, *The Universe Next Door*, 6th ed (Downers Grove: IVP Academic, 2020), Ch.1.

physical forces and in which death means extinction. Their Indian friend Bhavani believes in a universe in which there is a multiplicity of gods and demons and also believes that human beings undergo multiple reincarnations. Physically, Angela, Charles and Bhavani inhabit the same universe, but mentally the universes they inhabit are very different.

The fact that people's worldviews are different, and that they inhabit multiple different mental universes as a result, has consequences for people's behaviour. For example, in one person's universe, it may be wrong to eat animals at all; in a second person's universe, it may be wrong to eat pigs; while in a third person's universe, it may be fine to eat pork, but cows are off the menu. For another example, in one person's universe, marriage has to be between one man and one woman; in a second person's universe, a man may have multiple wives; and in a third person's universe, it may be fine for two people of the same sex to marry. A key challenge for a society such as the UK – where there is a plurality of worldviews – is therefore how people who hold different views on what constitutes right behaviour can learn to peacefully coexist, rather than being in constant conflict with one another.

The aim and shape of this book

The aim of this little book is to do three things.

- First, to explain the nature of the Christian universe and the reasons for believing that this universe exists not only as a mental concept, but as an objective reality.

- Secondly, to introduce Christians to the other main mental universes inhabited by people living in the UK and the reasons for their existence.

- Thirdly, to explore what it means for Christians to live well in the midst of these multiple mental universes.

I shall begin in chapter 1 by describing the orthodox Christian universe, using the Apostles' Creed as a starting point, and explaining the reasons for believing that this universe really exists as more than just a mental concept.

I shall then go on in chapters 2–4 to describe three other mental universes that have emerged since the seventeenth century on the basis of a deliberate rejection of the Christian universe and assess them from a Christian perspective. These are the deist, materialist and postmodern universes. After that I will go on in chapters 5–9 to look in turn at the Jewish, Islamic, Hindu, Buddhist and Sikh mental universes, also assessing them from a Christian perspective.

A key issue I shall consider in these chapters is what human flourishing means in these various different universes. The *New Oxford Dictionary of English* tells us that the verb 'to flourish' means 'to grow or develop in a healthy or vigorous way'. What this means exactly will vary according to what we are talking about.

In my garden, I have some rhubarb plants and also a population of wild rabbits. I can tell whether my rhubarb plants are flourishing by seeing whether or not they produce big green leaves and long red stems. If they do, the rhubarb is flourishing – but if they don't, then they are not. In the case of the rabbits, I can tell whether they are flourishing by seeing whether the individual rabbits are big and healthy, rather than small and sick, and whether they are producing lots of offspring. In both instances I have an idea of what it means for the plant or animal to be healthy or vigorous and I judge whether they are flourishing according to that yardstick.

As well as knowing something about what it means for plants and animals to flourish, all human beings have at least some basic ideas of what it means for human beings to flourish, even if this is not the term they would use. It is these ideas which shape the way human beings live their lives.

As the Canadian philosopher Charles Taylor notes in his book, *A Secular Age*:

> Every person, and every society, lives with or by some conception(s) of what human flourishing is: what constitutes a fulfilled life? What makes life really worth living? What would we most admire people for? We can't help asking these or related questions in our lives. And our struggles to answer them define the view or views that we try to live by, or between which we haver.[6]

We will consider what human flourishing means in the Christian universe. We will also look at what flourishing means in the other universes and how

6 Charles Taylor, *A Secular Age* (Cambridge MA: Belknap Press, 2007), 16.

their views of human flourishing compare with the Christian view.

In chapter 10, I shall address the question of why multiple mental universes exist by a giving a historical and theological overview of how and why different worldviews have developed since the first human cultures came into existence.

Finally, in chapter 11, I shall explore what it means to live well as a Christian in a country where these multiple universes now exist side by side. What is the right way for Christians to live in the multiverse? How should Christians relate to people who live in non-Christian universes? How should they go about trying to persuade them to come and inhabit the Christian universe instead?

In the two appendices at the end of the book I shall look at the answers given by Athanasius and C S Lewis to the question of why the incarnation needed to happen, and why we can be confident that it did, and at the argument by G K Chesterton that the Christian worldview reconciles the previously warring human tendencies to tell stories and to engage in a philosophical search for truth.

Anyone who knows the UK at all well will know that people live in lots of different universes that are not covered in this book. For instance, people live in Zoroastrian and Taoist universes, in various pagan and New Age universes, and, according to census returns, there are even a few Jedi knights living in the Star Wars universe (may the force be with them). The reason for not covering these universes is not because they are unimportant (on what basis would one make that decision?) but simply because keeping this book reasonably short has meant focusing on the universes which currently have the largest number of people inhabiting them.

1. The Christian Universe

A good starting point for understanding the Christian universe is the ancient Christian statement of faith known as the Apostles' Creed. In its present form, it can be traced back as far as the sixth century of the Christian era, but it is based on what is known as the Old Roman Creed, a statement of faith that can be traced back as far as the second century.[1]

The reason why the Apostles' Creed makes a good starting point for understanding the Christian universe is that it is a concise but comprehensive summary of the key elements of the teaching of the apostles (the first leaders appointed by Jesus Christ when he founded the Christian church), as found in the pages of the New Testament, the written record of the apostles' teaching.

As a summary of the apostles' teaching, the Apostles' Creed reflects what all the main branches of Christianity (Roman Catholic, Orthodox, Protestant and Pentecostal) have believed throughout the history of the church. It thus expresses the common core of Christian belief – what C S Lewis famously called 'mere Christianity'.[2]

The Apostles' Creed runs as follows:

> I believe in God, the Father almighty,
> creator of heaven and earth.

1 For more information about the history and development of the Apostles' Creed, see J. N. D. Kelly, *Early Christian Creeds*, 5th ed (London and New York: Continuum, 2000).
2 C. S. Lewis, Preface to *Mere Christianity* (Glasgow: Fount, 1984).

I believe in Jesus Christ, his only Son,
our Lord,
who was conceived by the Holy Spirit,
born of the Virgin Mary,
suffered under Pontius Pilate,
was crucified, died, and was buried;
he descended to the dead.
On the third day he rose again;
he ascended into heaven,
he is seated at the right hand
of the Father,
and he will come to judge the living
and the dead.

I believe in the Holy Spirit,
the holy catholic Church,
the communion of saints,
the forgiveness of sins,
the resurrection of the body,
and the life everlasting.
Amen.

The first thing we learn from the Apostles' Creed is that God exists, and that he exists in a particular way. In the Christian universe, there is one God who eternally exists as three persons (or personal conscious centres of existence) – God the Father, God the Son and God the Holy Spirit. (For the New Testament support for this belief, see Matthew 28:19, 2 Corinthians 13:14 and Revelation 1:4–5).

This Triune God is absolute (depending on nothing and no one else for his existence), personal, and omnipotent ('almighty') in the sense that he can do what he wills to do. Unlike human beings, God is also unlimited in his knowledge and his goodness.

We also learn from the Apostles' Creed both what God *has* done and what God *will* do. The three sections of the Creed describe in turn the activity of God the Father, God the Son and God the Holy Spirit in creating us, redeeming us and sanctifying us (making us holy). This activity is helpfully expounded by the sixteenth-century Protestant Reformer Martin Luther in his commentary on the Creed in his *Small Catechism* of 1529.

According to Luther, the first section of the Creed tells us:

> ...that God has created me and all that exists; that he has given me and still sustains my body and soul, all my limbs and senses, my reason and all the faculties of my mind, together with food and clothing, house and home, family and property; that he provides me daily and abundantly with all the necessities of life, protects me from all danger and preserves me from all evil. All this he does out of his pure, fatherly and divine goodness and mercy, without any merit or worthiness on my part.

The second section tells us:

> ...that Jesus Christ, true God, begotten of the Father from all eternity, and also true man, born of the virgin Mary, is my Lord, who has redeemed me, a lost and condemned creature, delivered me and freed me from all sins, from death and from the power of the devil, not with

silver and gold but with his holy and precious blood and with his innocent sufferings and death, in order that I may be his, live under him in his kingdom, and serve him in everlasting righteousness, innocence and blessedness, even as he is risen from the dead and lives and reigns to all eternity.

Finally, the third section tells us:

...that by my own reason or strength I cannot believe in Jesus Christ, my Lord, or come to him. But the Holy Spirit has called me through the gospel, enlightened me with his gifts, and sanctified and preserved me in true faith, just as he calls, gathers, enlightens and sanctifies the whole Christian church on earth and preserves it in union with Jesus Christ in the one true faith. In this Christian church he daily and abundantly forgives all my sins, and the sins of all believers, and on the last day he will raise me and all the dead and will grant eternal life to me and all who believe in Christ, this is most certainly true.[3]

What Luther does not say, but the New Testament and the wider Christian tradition do say, is that the those who have been resurrected to eternal life will live forever in 'a new heaven and a new earth'

---

3 Martin Luther, Small Catechism, II, in Mark Noll ed., *Confessions and Catechisms of the Reformation* (Vancouver: Regent College Publishing, 2004), 68–69.

"The Christian faith gives us answers to a series of key questions which can be addressed to all worldviews"

Christian
Jewish Islamic
multiverse
postmodern
materialist
Living
well
deist
Hindu
Sik

(Revelation 21:1). As a result of rebellion against God by the devil and by human beings under his influence, the present creation is infected with sin and heading towards death, but God will make it new again with an existence in which sin, suffering and death are no more and in which Christians will share in his just rule over creation in the way he has always intended they should (see Genesis 1:26-28).

What Luther also does not say, because he is addressing believers, is that the judgement of the living and the dead referred to in the Creed will have a dual outcome. Those who have believed in Christ and have been sanctified by his Spirit will enjoy a blessed eternity, but those who persist in rejecting God's love to the end of their lives will be separated from God and all that is good for ever (Daniel 12:2, Matthew 25:31–46, Revelation 20:11–15). In the words of the evangelical theologian J I Packer, 'The unbeliever has preferred to be by himself, without God, defying God, having God against him, and he shall have his choice.'[4]

What all this means is that the Christian faith gives us answers to a series of key questions which can be addressed to all worldviews.

The first question is **'Why am I here?'** In the Christian universe, the answer to this question is that I and everything else that exists (including the spiritual beings which the Bible and the Christian tradition call 'angels') are in existence because we have been created and are sustained by God.

---

4 J. I. Packer, *Knowing God* (London: Hodder and Stoughton, 1973), 161.

The second question is **'Who am I?'** In the Christian universe, the answer which I can give to this question if I am a Christian believer is that I am someone made up of material body and an immaterial soul, whom God has created, redeemed and sanctified.

The third question is **'How should I live?'** In the Christian universe, the answer is that I should be a believer and therefore I should live as someone whom God has created, redeemed and sanctified (with the Old and New Testaments in the Bible instructing me as to what this should mean in practice).

It is important to note that in the Bible and the Christian tradition, the ethics that flow from God's activity in creation, redemption and sanctification are one and the same. For example, the creation accounts in the book of Genesis in the Old Testament tell us that God established lifelong marriage between one man and one woman as the proper setting for sexual intercourse and the begetting and rearing of children (Genesis 1:28, 2:18–25). As Christians who have been redeemed and sanctified, we are summoned and enabled to live in this way (1 Thessalonians 4:1–8, Ephesians 5:21–6:4).

The fourth question is **'What may I hope for?'** In the Christian universe, the answer is that I may hope that I shall fulfil the destiny for which I was created by living and reigning joyfully with God forever in body and soul in the new creation that God is going to bring into existence.

What all this means is that in the Christian universe, flourishing as a human being means living in this world in accordance with the instruction given in the Bible, as someone whom God has created, redeemed and sanctified, and then living joyfully with God forever in the world to come.

If that is the Christian universe, what are the reasons for believing that this is a universe that really exists as more than just a mental concept, that it is, to coin a phrase 'really real'?

There are three reasons for believing this.

First, if the Christian universe really exists it provides answers to otherwise unanswerable questions about our existence.

- It tells us why we exist in a world and a cosmos that bears the marks of design (because we have been created by an intelligent creator God).

- It tells us why we have an ineradicable sense that there is a difference between right and wrong (because we were created by God to live in a particular way).

- It tells us why we think there is something wrong with the world and with ourselves (because there is – we have rebelled against God under the influence of the devil and we suffer alienation from God, from each other, and from the created order, and are subject to death as a result).

- It tells us why we have a desire for joy that can never be fully fulfilled in this world (because we were created for the eternal joy which we will only experience in relationship with God in the new creation).

Secondly, the evidence of history tells us that there really was a people called Israel who existed from the time of Abraham. God promised them that he would send someone descended from the Israelite King David who would deliver the world from sin and death and rule over the world in righteousness on God's behalf, and that he would renew the life of his people though the gift of the Holy Spirit (Psalm 110:1–7, Isaiah 11:1–9, Joel 2:28–29). It also tells us that this promise was fulfilled by God through the incarnation, life, death, resurrection and ascension of Jesus Christ, and the pouring out of the Spirit on the day of Pentecost (Acts 2:1–36).

Thirdly, God himself testifies to his own existence and activity in the Bible. God inspired the writers of the Bible through the Holy Spirit so that what they wrote bore faithful witness to God's being and activity (2 Timothy 3:16, 2 Peter 1:21) and he illuminates our hearts through that same Spirit so that we are enabled to perceive and accept the truth of the biblical message (1 Corinthians 2:6–16, 2 Corinthians 3:12–4:6).

Having looked at the Christian universe and the reasons for believing it to be 'really real' we will go on in the next chapter to look at the deist universe, which developed as an alternative to the Christian universe from the late seventeenth century onwards.

2. The Deist Universe

Scholars continue to debate the precise meaning of the term deism and there is controversy about which historical figures should be counted as deists. However, what is beyond doubt is that from the end of the seventeenth century onwards there was an intellectual movement in Western Europe and North America that wanted to retain belief in God while abandoning many of the key beliefs of orthodox Christianity in both its Protestant and Roman Catholic forms. Among those who formed part of this intellectual movement were John Toland, Matthew Tindal and William Wollaston in Britain, Thomas Jefferson in America, Voltaire in France, and Hermann Reimarus in Germany.[1]

This intellectual movement seems to have had three origins.

The first was a desire to find a unifying alternative to the opposing Protestant and Roman Catholic theological traditions that had emerged out of the Reformation. All of them claimed to teach the truth about God and his ways, but all vehemently disagreed with each other – a disagreement which had led to war across Europe during the course of the seventeenth century.

The second was a growing confidence in the power of unaided human reason to discover truth. This confidence was inspired by the growing success of the use of reason in understanding the natural world.

---

1 For an accessible introduction to the debate about the meaning of deism, see Sire, *Universe Next Door*, Ch.3.

The third was the influence of the picture of the universe that seemed to emerge from the use of reason in investigating the natural world. In the words of James Sire: 'A picture of God's world began to emerge, it was seen to be like a huge, well-ordered mechanism, a giant clockwork, whose gears and levers meshed with perfect mechanical precision.'[2]

Out of the combination of these three factors, a distinctive worldview eventually emerged. It envisaged a different universe from that depicted in orthodox Christianity in either its Protestant or Roman Catholic forms. The key features of this universe were as follows:

- There is a supernatural entity, 'God,' who designed the universe and brought it into being.

- Having created the universe, God left it to run its course. God has no cause to tinker with the operation of the perfect mechanism he has created.

- It follows that religious traditions (such as orthodox Christianity) and religious texts (such as the Bible) which declare that God has intervened in the universe must be mistaken. It also means that Jesus cannot have been God incarnate nor the Spirit sent down by God at Pentecost.

- Morality is to be determined by the reflection of reason upon the nature of human existence since what is good

2 Sire, *Universe Next Door*, Kindle edition, 36–37.

is for human beings to act according to their created nature.

- There may or may not be life after physical death.

The French historian Emile Bréhier helpfully sums up the difference between this view of the universe and the traditional Christian view when he writes:

> We see clearly that a new conception of man, wholly incompatible with the Christian faith, has been introduced: God the architect who produced and maintained a marvellous order in the universe had been discovered in nature, and there was no longer a place for the God of the Christian drama, the God who bestowed upon Adam 'the power to sin and to reverse the order.' God was in nature and no longer in history; he was in the wonders analyzed by naturalists and biologists and no longer in the human conscience, with feelings of sin, disgrace, or grace that accompanied his presence; he had left man in charge of his own destiny.[3]

Deism as an explicit theological and philosophical position had its heyday in the eighteenth century. However, there are still a very large number of people in Britain today who are deists (even if they would not use the term to describe themselves) and who would see themselves as inhabiting the kind of universe described in the bullet points listed above.

---

3 Emile Bréhier, *The History of Philosophy* (Chicago: Chicago University Press, 1967), 5:15.

They would acknowledge the existence of some first cause or higher power, but they would not accept that God has intervened in the world in the way described by orthodox Christianity. They would also be unclear about whether there is a life after death. Furthermore, they would hold that ethics should be determined by rational reflection upon the nature of human existence rather than by the teaching of the Bible or the church.

A modern variant of the deistic position that is held by very many people, including many who would describe themselves as Christians, is what is known as 'moralistic therapeutic deism.' This term was coined by the American sociologists Christian Smith and Melinda Lundquist Denton to describe the worldview uncovered by their 2005 study of the beliefs of American teenagers. They summarised this worldview as follows:

1. A God exists who created and orders the world and watches over human life on earth.

2. God wants people to be good, nice and fair to each other as taught in the Bible and by most religions.

3. The central goal of life is to be happy and to feel good about oneself.

4. God does not need to be particularly involved in one's life except when God is needed to resolve a problem.

5. Good people go to heaven when they die.[4]

In the deist universe, human flourishing means living in the way that we think is best as determined by rational reflection on the nature of human life as created by God. In the 'moralistic therapeutic' version of deism, living in this way means living in way that makes us happy and makes us feel good about ourselves. A life lived in this way may or may not find fulfilment in a new life after death.

A Christian view of the Deist universe

From a Christian perspective, the first version of deism described above is correct when it says that God designed and created the world. Where it errs is in insisting that God takes a 'hands off' approach thereafter. The Christian response to this error can be set out as follows.

First, the general regularity of the natural order cannot rule out God intervening supernaturally if he has good reason for doing so.

Secondly, looking at the state of the world shows us that it is not true that, as the eighteenth-century English writer Alexander Pope famously put it in his work *An Essay on Man*, 'One truth is clear, whatever is, is right.'[5] For Christianity, the presence of evil and

---

4 Christian Smith and Melinda Lundquist Denton, *Soul Searching: The Religious and Spiritual Lives of American Teenagers* (New York: OUP, 2005), 162–163.
5 Alexander Pope, *An Essay on Man* (Indianapolis and New York: Bobs-Merrill, 1965), Epistle 1, Line 294.

death in the world show that this is not the case. There are some things that are that should not be.

Thirdly, the best explanation for the existence of evil and death in the world is that given by orthodox Christianity – namely, that a supernatural anti-God force (the devil) has acted in a way that has brought evil into the world, with death as evil's eventual result.

Fourthly, this being the case, there is good reason for God to intervene in the world in order to counter the results of the devil's activity.

Fifthly, the witness of Scripture, which there is every reason to trust, is that God has in fact intervened for this reason, and that because of this intervention, life after death is not simply probable but certain.

Finally, while it is true that ethics should be rooted in the created nature of human beings, what that nature is has to be carefully discerned in a way that screens out the corruption that has entered into the world and by which human nature and the human mind is now infected.

In relation to 'moralistic therapeutic deism' orthodox Christianity would say 'yes' to point 1 in the list of its five main tenets given above. It would also say 'yes' to point 2 – with the proviso that because of the intellectual confusion and moral weakness resulting from the devil's corruption of human nature, people need God's help to understand what it means to be 'good, nice and fair' to others and God's strength to have the desire and ability to do it.

On point 3 orthodox Christianity would agree that

God's long-term intention is that we should indeed be happy and feel good about ourselves. In the world to come, both will be the case. However, in this world the corruption of our nature by the devil means that we should not feel good about who we are because, to quote the *Book of Common Prayer*, 'We have left undone those things which we ought to have done, and we have done those things which we ought not to have done, And there is no health in us.' Furthermore, in order to become the people God created us to be we have to be prepared to 'put to death' all those evil desires and activities that stem from the corruption of our nature (Colossians 3:5). Doing this will not necessarily cause us immediate happiness. In fact, in the short term it may make us very unhappy indeed. However, the long-term reward will be worth it.

On point 4, for the reasons given in relation to point 2, we need God to be present and at work in our lives through his Spirit all the time and not just an occasional moment of crisis.

On point 5, orthodox Christianity would agree that 'good people go to heaven when they die.' However, it would go on to say that the goodness of such people will be what Christian theology calls an 'alien righteousness.' No human being, with the exception of Jesus Christ, has ever been, or will ever be, truly and consistently good. 'All have sinned and fall short of the glory of God' (Romans 3:23). For that reason, no one, in their natural state, is capable of going to heaven. However, God has dealt with this situation. In Jesus Christ, God brought about what Luther called a 'marvellous exchange.' He took our sinful nature upon himself and put it to death on the cross and he rose to give us a new holy nature in its place (Romans 6:1–11). When we believe and are baptised, what Jesus did for us becomes real in us through the work of the Holy Spirit and so we become people who are fit to live for ever with God after we die.[6]

Deism and Christianity on human flourishing

In terms of their views of human flourishing, the key point of difference between deism and Christianity is that in deism it is human beings who have to decide what flourishing means and who then have to try to live in this way on the basis of their own unaided moral resources. In Christianity, God reveals what flourishing means and it is he who also gives us the ability to live in this way.

In addition, in Christianity, human flourishing finds its culmination in a life lived with God in the world to come – whereas in some forms of deism, human flourishing is limited solely to what happens in this world.

6 See Martin Luther, 'The Freedom of a Christian' in Martin Luther, *Three Treatises* (Philadelphia: Fortress Press, 1978).

"In Christianity, God reveals what flourishing means and it is he who also gives us the ability to live in this way."

3. The Materialist Universe

The materialist universe can be seen as a further development of the deist universe described in the last chapter. The reason for calling this universe 'materialist' is that, like the Ancient Greek philosopher Democritus who believed that the universe was made up of material bodies which he called atoms, those who inhabit it hold that nothing exists except the materials of which the physical universe is made up. There is nothing that is non-material.

As we have seen, in the deist universe God's role is reduced to that of designing and creating the universe. In the materialist universe God loses even that role. This point is illustrated if we compare the ideas of the eighteenth- and nineteenth-century Christian apologist William Paley with the thought of the contemporary materialist writer Richard Dawkins.

In his book *Natural Theology*, published in 1802, Paley wrote as follows:

> In crossing a heath, suppose I pitched my foot against a stone, and were asked how the stone came to be there; I might possibly answer, that, for anything I knew to the contrary, it had lain there forever: nor would it perhaps be very easy to show the absurdity of this answer. But suppose I had found a watch upon the ground, and it should be inquired how the watch happened to be in that place; I should hardly think of the answer I

had before given, that for anything I knew, the watch might have always been there.... There must have existed, at some time, and at some place or other, an artificer or artificers, who formed [the watch] for the purpose which we find it actually to answer; who comprehended its construction, and designed its use.... Every indication of contrivance, every manifestation of design, which existed in the watch, exists in the works of nature; with the difference, on the side of nature, of being greater or more, and that in a degree which exceeds all computation.[1]

Paley's point is simple. Just as we are justified in deducing the existence of a watchmaker from the existence of a watch, so we are even more justified in deducing the existence of a creator – God – from the world that he has made.

By contrast, in his 1986 book, *The Blind Watchmaker*, Dawkins writes: 'Natural selection is the blind watchmaker, blind because it does not see ahead, does not plan consequences, has no purpose in view.'[2] For Dawkins the watchmaker is not God, but the blind forces of natural selection.

Dawkins's reference to 'natural selection' is key to understanding the shift from deism to materialism. The reason that deists believed in God was that they

1 William Paley, *Natural Theology*, Chapters I and III at https://faculty.uca.edu/benw/biol4415/papers/paley1.pdf
2 Richard Dawkins, *The Blind Watchmaker* (New York: W.W. Norton, 1986), 21.

thought, like Paley, that the complex mechanism of nature required God as the 'artificer' who designed and created it. With the development of the theory of evolution by Charles Darwin and others in the nineteenth century it seemed to many people that God's role had become redundant. The blind forces of nature operating through a process of natural selection could explain perfectly well how life on earth developed without reference to God, and by extension such forces could also explain how the universe as a whole developed. Hence materialism.

If we ask what sort of a universe is envisaged by those who hold a materialist worldview, the answer is helpfully given by the materialist philosopher Bertrand Russell. In his 'Litany of Despair', he declares that within a materialist frame of reference we must accept:

> ...that man is the product of causes which had no prevision of the end they were achieving; that his origin, his growth, his hopes and fears, his loves and his beliefs are but the outcomes of accidental collocations of atoms; that no fire, no heroism, no intensity of thought and feeling, can preserve an individual life beyond the grave; that all the labours of the ages, all the devotion, all the inspiration, all the noonday brightness of human genius, are destined to extinction in the vast death of the solar system, and that the whole temple of man's achievement must inevitably be buried beneath the debris of a universe in ruins

– all these things, if not quite beyond dispute, are yet so nearly certain that no philosophy which rejects them can hope to stand. Only within the scaffolding of these truths, only in the firm foundation of unyielding despair, can the soul's habitation henceforth be safely built.[3]

To return to the worldview questions that we looked at in chapter 1 in relation to the Christian universe, what we can see is that in the materialist universe described by Russell, the answer to the question 'Why am I here?' is 'For no reason at all.' The answer to the question 'Who am I?' is 'I am an accidental collocation of atoms without meaning or purpose.'

Russell does not address the issue 'How should I live?' but a representative account of what ethics look like in a materialist universe is provided by the second *Humanist Manifesto* issued by the American Humanist Association in 1973. This states:

> We affirm that moral values derive their sources from human experience. Ethics is *autonomous* and *situational*, needing no theological or ideological sanctions. Ethics stems from human need and interest. To deny this distorts the whole basis of life. Human life has meaning because we create and develop our futures.[4]

3 Bertrand Russell, *Mysticism and Logic* (New York: Barnes and Noble, 1917), 47–48.
4 American Humanist Association, *Humanist Manifesto II* at: https://americanhumanist.org/what-is-humanism/manifesto2/.

What this statement tells us is that for the materialist there is no transcendent, supernatural, source of authority for ethics. Ethics is about how autonomous human beings choose to live their lives. The answer to the question 'How should I live?' is 'In whatever way seems right to me.'

In terms of human flourishing, materialists hold that physical death is the end of human existence and so flourishing means flourishing solely in this world. Because there is no meaning or plan in the material order, human beings have to decide what flourishing in this world means for them.

To quote Charles Taylor again, in the materialist universe:

> Everyone has a right to develop their own form of life, grounded on their own sense of what is really important or of value. People are called upon to be true to themselves and to seek their own self-fulfilment. What this consists of, each must, in the last instance, determine for him- or herself. No one else can or should try to dictate its content.[5]

Christianity and the materialist universe

From a Christian perspective there are a number of key problems with the materialist worldview.

First, the basic foundation of the materialist

---

5 Charles Taylor, *The Ethics of Authenticity* (Cambridge MA: Harvard University Press, 1992), 14.

worldview, that the findings of science leave no place for God, is untenable. What we continue to learn about the world and the cosmos tells us that Paley was right after all. As the American scientist Stephen Meyer puts it in his recent book, *The Return of the God Hypothesis*:

> Not only does theism solve a lot of philosophical problems, but empirical evidence from the material world points powerfully to the reality of a great mind behind the universe. Our beautiful, expanding, and finely tuned universe, and the exquisite, integrated and informational complexity of living organisms bear witness to the reality of a transcendent intelligence – a personal God.[6]

Secondly, materialism's account of human nature undermines itself. If, as Russell suggests, human thought is simply the product of the random movement of atoms, which has been produced in turn by previous random movements of atoms back to the dawn of time, then I have no reason for believing that my belief about the nature of human thought is true. As John Haldane puts it: 'If my mental processes are determined wholly by the motions of atoms in my brain, I have no reason to suppose my belief is true.'[7] Only if there is a rational creator, God, who has created his creatures with rational souls, do we have

6 Stephen Meyer, *The Return of the God Hypothesis* (London: Harper Collins, 2021), Kindle edition, 517.
7 John Haldane, 'When I am Dead' in *Possible Worlds and Other Essays* (London: Chatto and Windus, 1927), 209.

"Only if there is a
rational creator, God,
who has created his creatures
with rational souls,
do we have any reason
to have confidence
in our powers of reason."

Christian
Jewish Islamic
multiverse
postmodern
materialist
Living
well
deist
Hindu

any reason to have confidence in our powers of reason and thus any confidence in our ability to understand the nature of the universe that we inhabit.

Thirdly, materialism's account of ethics is vulnerable to what the Yale professor Arthur Leff has called 'the great sez who.'[8] The point is that if right and wrong are simply a human construct, then if anyone says, 'You should do this,' or 'You should not do that,' then the obvious response is to reply, 'Says who?' If there is no transcendent moral authority which stands above the ideas and desires of human beings, then there is no basis on which to say that there are some things which should be done and some which should not. However, materialists do not generally accept the logic of their own position on this matter. They, like other human beings, still want to say that there are things that are just simply wrong.

However, the only way we can make sense of the universal human belief that some things are right and some things are simply wrong is if we were created by a God who is absolutely good in himself and who has given us the ability to understand what it means for us to reflect his goodness in the way we behave.

Fourthly, those who are Christians know that materialism is wrong because God has revealed himself in the history of Israel and in the person of Jesus Christ to be 'a living and true God' (1 Thessalonians 1:9) and has borne witness to that revelation through his word in the Bible and through

8 Tom Leinbach, 'The Grand 'Sez Who'.' *Climbing the Walls*, April 18, 2018 at https://climbingthewalls.org/the-grand-sez-who/.

his Spirit who seals the truth of this witness in our hearts. If I reveal myself to you then you know that I exist. Likewise with God.

Materialism and Christianity on human flourishing

There are two fundamental points of difference between materialism and Christianity with regard to human flourishing.

First, as we have noted, for the materialist flourishing is something which can happen only in this world since human existence ceases at death. For the Christian, human flourishing, while beginning in this world, finds its culmination in the life of the world to come.

Secondly, the materialist, like the deist, holds that each person has to decide for themselves what flourishing means and has to find the resources within themselves to live in that way. In the Christian universe, by contrast, it is God who both makes known to us what flourishing means and gives us the ability to flourish in this way.

4. The Postmodern Universe

Postmodernism is an intellectual movement that began in the twentieth century and is associated with figures such as Jacques Derrida, Michel Foucault, Jean-François Lyotard and Richard Rorty.

In a book published in 1979 called *The Postmodern Condition*, Lyotard famously described postmodernism as 'incredulity towards metanarratives.'[1] What he meant was that postmodernists reject the idea that there is one view of things that describes the world as it really is, whether that view of things is Christianity, materialism or anything else.

Postmodernism is called *post*modernism because it is an intellectual movement that followed on after modernism but rejected the belief central to modernism that human beings could give a truthful account of the world through the use of reason.

In the postmodern universe, the accepted view of things is that what we think of as truth is determined by the prevailing story told by a society or institution. Thus, Americans may believe that it is true that America is 'the land of the free and the home of the brave' but the reason they believe this to be true is because of the prevailing story told in American society and reinforced by the singing of the American national anthem.

---

1 Jean-François Lyotard, *The Postmodern Condition* (Minneapolis: University of Minnesota Press, 1984), 24.

The reason such stories are told, according to postmodern theory, is in order to serve the ends of those with power in any given society or institution. In the words of Kevin Vanhoozer, for those who subscribe to a postmodernist worldview, truth is 'a compelling story told by persons in positions of power in order to perpetuate their way of seeing and organising the natural and social world.'[2] For example, the traditional idea that kings and queens have power bestowed on them by God is, from a postmodern viewpoint, simply a story told by monarchs and their supporters to justify their exercise of political power.

The postmodern scepticism about truth extends across all intellectual disciplines. Thus, in history there is no one view of the past that is more truthful than any other, there is simply a collection of stories people tell about the past. Likewise in science there is no one correct way of understanding the world, there is just a collection of stories that people tell in order to make sense of the world or to achieve certain ends, such as making things that work. Similarly, in literature there is no one meaning of a text, simply different accounts of the text by different readers or group of readers. 'What does Jane Austen's *Pride and Prejudice* mean?' is a meaningless question.

Furthermore, in the postmodern universe there is nothing that is natural. What is 'natural' is simply what is seen as natural in the context of a particular story. For instance, the distinction between 'normal'

2 Kevin Vanhoozer, 'Theology and the condition of postmodernity' in Kevin Vanhoozer, ed., *The Cambridge Companion to Postmodern Theology* (Cambridge: CUP, 2003), 11.

behaviour and 'madness' only exists in relation to the account of human behaviour contained in the stories that are told about being human. People are 'normal' or 'mad' because that is how these stories describes them. In similar fashion, what is right or wrong is determined by the stories told by those in power. To quote James Sire, in postmodernism 'the good is whatever those who wield the power in society choose to make it.'[3]

Most radically of all, postmodernism deconstructs the self. Since the work of the French philosopher René Descartes in the seventeenth century, the one thing that the Western world has reckoned it could be sure about is the existence of the self that knows itself and the world around it. Whatever else may be uncertain, that point is seen as certain. In Descartes' words 'Cogito ergo sum - I think therefore I am.' However, as Vanhoozer notes: 'Postmoderns do not believe in the metanarrative of the knowing subject. The postmodern self is not master of, but subject to, the material and social and linguistic conditions of a historical situation that precedes her.'[4]

In order to unpack Vanhoozer's point, we can imagine a nineteenth-century domestic servant called Mabel. If you asked Mabel who she was, the way she would understand and describe herself would be shaped by the society of which she was a part and the understandings of class and sex present in that society. The conclusion postmodernists would draw from this is that Mabel is a social and linguistic

---

3 Sire, *Universe Next Door*, 217.
4 Vanhoozer, 'Theology and condition and postmodernity', 12.

construct. There is no Mabel except the Mabel who is constructed by the stories told in her society.

What are known as 'critical theories' about sex, gender and race that have become so prevalent in contemporary academia can best be seen as a political development of postmodern thought. In the words of Helen Pluckrose and James Lindsay, critical theories arose as an 'applied turn' of postmodern theory.[5] To misquote Karl Marx, postmodernists had described the world, but critical theorists sought to change it.

To quote Pluckrose and Lindsay again:

> During its applied turn, [postmodern] Theory underwent a *moral* mutation: it adopted a number of beliefs about the rights and wrongs of power and privilege. The original theorists were content to observe, bemoan, and play with such phenomena; the new ones wanted to reorder society. If social injustice is caused by legitimising bad discourses, they reasoned, social justice can be achieved by delegitimising them and replacing them with better ones.[6]

According to postmodern critical theorists, discourses produced by those who are white, male, straight, cisgender (in other words, have a gender identity that corresponds with their biological sex) and who are not physically or mentally disabled are

5 Helen Pluckrose and James Lindsay, *Cynical Theories* (London: Swift Press, 2020), Ch.2.
6 Pluckrose and Lindsay, *Cynical Theories*, Kindle edition, 54.

bad because they lead to the oppression of those who are not these things. The oppressive nature of these discourses needs to be uncovered and they need to be replaced by discourses reflecting the experiences and concerns of the oppressed. In this way society can be changed for the better.

There are two views of human flourishing in postmodernism.

On the one hand, the basic postmodern scepticism towards all truth claims means that theoretically there can be no such thing as a truthful account of human flourishing. Flourishing means whatever it means within the prevailing discourse of a particular social group.

On the other hand, postmodern critical theorists argue very strongly that oppressive forms of discourse need to be done away with in order that society can be changed for the better. This latter argument suggests that some ways of ordering society are more conducive to human flourishing than others and that therefore such a thing as flourishing does really exist.

If we ask critical theorists how we know what flourishing looks like, their answer is that this is determined by the experiences and needs of the oppressed. It is for them to say what they need in order to flourish.

Christianity and the postmodern universe

From a Christian perspective, there are elements of truth in the postmodern worldview and in the critical theory that has flowed from it. It is undoubtedly true that how we understand ourselves is shaped by the stories that are told in the societies to which we belong. It is also undoubtedly true that people use language to support their own power and privilege and to oppress other people and that this is something which needs to be challenged.

However, like materialism, postmodernism undermines itself. In its purest form, postmodernism holds that all language is simply a power play and as such is incapable of leading us to grasp the objective truth about ourselves or the world in which we live. To put it simply, for the consistent postmodernist, the truth is that there is no truth (or at least no truth that we can know). Unfortunately for the postmodernist, this also means that we have no reason to believe that postmodernism is true. The postmodernists have created for themselves a universe in which their own beliefs cannot be justified.

In the Christian universe, by contrast, the creator God knows truth about things (in the words of Job 28:24, God 'looks to the ends of the earth and sees everything under heaven') and is able to communicate that truth effectively to his creatures. He speaks through nature and Scripture and enables us to know the truth about God, ourselves, and the world in which we live. He also gives us the ability to communicate this truth to each other.

The highest example of this is Scripture, which is an act of human communication that conveys the truth that God wanted to impart. However, there are innumerable other examples of truthful communication as well, something that we simply take for granted in our day-to-day living. To give three random examples, truth is communicated to us through weather forecasts, traffic reports and train timetables.

Because we are creatures who are both finite and fallen, we are ignorant of the truth about many things, and we are not always willing to accept the truth when it is made known to us. We also fail, accidentally or deliberately, to communicate the truth that we do know to others. All this is undeniable. However, the point is that that the postmodern claim that we can never know the truth or communicate involves a blanket scepticism which is unjustified and which, as we have seen, undermines itself.

In similar fashion, from a Christian perspective postmodernism is also mistaken when it attempts to deconstruct the self. Of course, the way we understand ourselves is shaped by the stories that are told in the societies of which we are a part. However, the point is that *there is something to understand*. We really exist as people created by God and redeemed through Christ. The challenge we face is, through the use of our minds and with God's assistance, to grow in a truthful understanding of who we are and how we should live in consequence.

Moving on to the critical theorists, what we find is that, while they are very clear that certain forms of language and behaviour are oppressive, what they are not clear about is how they know this is the case. Like postmodernism as a whole, critical theory accepts as given a materialist view of the universe and for the reasons given in the previous chapter, it is therefore unable to offer as satisfying explanation as to why some things are oppressive and some are not, or why oppression is wrong in the first place. Why is it wrong for some people to be racist if they feel that is what is right for them? Critical theory cannot tell us.

In addition, critical theorists falsely divide the world into two. There are the oppressors (those who are white, male, straight, cisgender and normally abled) and there are the oppressed (those who are non-white, female, gay, transgender and disabled). The former are the villains and the latter are their hapless innocent victims. From a Christian point of view, this binary analysis fails to acknowledge the truth that 'all have sinned and fall short of the glory of God' (Romans 3:23) and therefore all mistreat others through their speech and actions. It also fails to acknowledge that through the grace of God all types of people can and do act virtuously. There are thus not two classes of human beings, the oppressed and the oppressors, but a single class of human beings who act sinfully or virtuously in a whole variety of different ways.

Furthermore, from a Christian perspective, some of the things that critical theorists claim are oppressive are not actually oppressive at all. Thus, it is not oppressive to say that people should live according to their biological sex or should not have sex with someone of their own sex because the witness of both nature and Scripture tells us that both statements reflect the reality of who human beings are and how God wants them to live in consequence. God created human beings as male and female creatures (Genesis 1:26–28) who are designed to have sex with members of the opposite sex in the context of marriage (Genesis 2:18–25) and it is not oppressive to say that

"The challenge we face is, through the use of our minds and with God's assistance, to grow in a truthful understanding of who we are and how we should live in consequence."

Christian
Jewish Islamic
multiverse
postmodern
materialist
Living
well
deist
Hindu

this is the case.

Postmodernism and Christianity on human flourishing

The ways in which postmodern and Christian accounts of human flourishing differ depends on what form of postmodernism you are talking about.

Some sceptical postmodern theorists want to say there is no truthful account of human flourishing, only the stories about flourishing contained in the discourses of particular social groups. In contrast, Christianity says that there is a truthful metanarrative, or overarching story, about human flourishing, a metanarrative that carries the authority of the 'God who never lies' (Titus 1:2) and which is contained in the Bible.

In contrast to the postmodern critical theorists who argue that it is for the oppressed to determine what flourishing means, Christianity says that the claims about flourishing made by members of oppressed groups have to be critically assessed in the light of the biblical metanarrative in order to decide which should be accepted and which should not.

In addition, a study of the works of postmodern critical theorists shows that their vision of flourishing for the oppressed is limited to their flourishing in this world, whereas, as we have seen Christianity insists that a truthful account of human flourishing has to include eternal flourishing in the world to come.

5. The Jewish Universe

According to traditional Jewish law, someone is Jewish if their mother is Jewish, or if both parents were both non-Jewish but have converted to Judaism in a way that accords with Jewish law. Jews who are non-religious either in their belief or their practice are still considered Jewish. According to the Talmud, the ancient collection of rabbinic teaching, 'A Jew, although he has transgressed, is still a Jew' (Sanhedrin 44a).

What this means is that there are today numerous secular Jews who hold to a deist, materialist, or postmodern worldview. Nevertheless, there is also a distinctively Jewish worldview to which those who inhabit a Jewish religious universe adhere. The core of this worldview is summarised by the words of the Shema, the oldest statement of faith in the Jewish tradition. The Shema is sometimes referred to as a prayer, but it is not actually a prayer, but a recitation of three passages from the Torah (the first five books of the Hebrew Bible), which have been recited by Jewish people day and night since ancient times.

The first is Deuteronomy 6:4–9:

> Hear, O Israel: The LORD our God is one LORD; and you shall love the LORD your God with all your heart, and with all your soul, and with all your might. And these words which I command you this day shall be upon your heart; and you shall teach them diligently to your children, and shall talk of them when you sit in your

house, and when you walk by the way, and when you lie down, and when you rise. And you shall bind them as a sign upon your hand, and they shall be as frontlets between your eyes. And you shall write them on the doorposts of your house and on your gates.

The second is Deuteronomy 11:13–21:

And if you will obey my commandments which I command you this day, to love the Lord your God, and to serve him with all your heart and with all your soul, he will give the rain for your land in its season, the early rain and the later rain, that you may gather in your grain and your wine and your oil. And he will give grass in your fields for your cattle, and you shall eat and be full. Take heed lest your heart be deceived, and you turn aside and serve other gods and worship them, and the anger of the Lord be kindled against you, and he shut up the heavens, so that there be no rain, and the land yield no fruit, and you perish quickly off the good land which the Lord gives you.

You shall therefore lay up these words of mine in your heart and in your soul; and you shall bind them as a sign upon your hand, and they shall be as frontlets between your eyes. And you shall teach them to your children, talking of them when you are sitting in your house, and when you are walking by the way, and when you lie down, and when you rise. And you shall write them upon the doorposts of your house and upon your gates, that your days and the days of your children may be multiplied in the land which the LORD swore to your fathers to give them, as long as the heavens are above the earth.

The third is Numbers 15:37–41:

The LORD said to Moses, 'Speak to the people of Israel, and bid them to make tassels on the corners of their garments throughout their generations, and to put upon the tassel of each corner a cord of blue; and it shall be to you a tassel to look upon and remember all the commandments of the LORD, to do them, not to follow after your own heart and your own eyes, which you are inclined to go after wantonly. So you shall remember and do all my commandments, and be holy to your God. I am the LORD your God, who brought you out of the land of Egypt, to be your God: I am the LORD your God.'

What we see in these three passages is belief in one God who has brought his people Israel out of the land of Egypt and who calls them to worship him alone, to love him with all of their being, and to live as holy people in obedience to his commandments, given by God to Moses (and recorded in the books of the Torah), with a promise of blessing if they do so, and of judgement if they do not.

An expanded form of the theology set out in the Shema is contained in the 'thirteen principles of faith' developed in the twelfth century by the Jewish writer Maimonides.[1] These principles run as follows:

1. I believe with perfect faith that the Creator, Blessed be His Name, is the Creator and Guide of everything that has been created; He alone has made, does make and will make all things.

2. I believe with perfect faith that the Creator, Blessed be His Name, is One, and that there is no unity in any manner like His, and that He alone is our God, who was, and is, and will be.

3. I believe with perfect faith that the Creator, Blessed be His Name, has no body, and that He is free from all the properties of matter, and that there can be no (physical) comparison to Him whatsoever.

4. I believe with perfect faith that the Creator, Blessed be His Name, is the first and the last.

5. I believe with perfect faith that to the Creator, Blessed be His Name, and to Him alone, it is right to pray, and that it is not right to pray to any being besides Him.

---

1 For an introduction to Maimonides and his significance, see Alberto Manguel, *Maimonides: Faith in Reason (Jewish Lives)* (New Haven: Yale University Press, 2023).

6. I believe with perfect faith that all the words of the prophets are true.

7. I believe with perfect faith that the prophecy of Moses our teacher, peace be upon him, was true, and that he was the chief of the prophets, both those who preceded him and those who followed him.

8. I believe with perfect faith that the entire Torah that is now in our possession is the same that was given to Moses our teacher, peace be upon him.

9. I believe with perfect faith that this Torah will not be exchanged and that there will never be any other Torah from the Creator, Blessed be His Name.

10. I believe with perfect faith that the Creator, Blessed be His Name, knows all the deeds of human beings and all their thoughts, as it is written, 'Who fashioned the hearts of them all, Who comprehends all their actions' (Psalm 33:15).

11. I believe with perfect faith that the Creator, Blessed be His Name, rewards those who keep His commandments and punishes those that transgress them.

12. I believe with perfect faith in the coming of the Messiah; and even

though he may tarry, nonetheless, I
wait every day for his coming.

13. I believe with perfect faith that there
will be a revival of the dead at the
time when it shall please the Creator,
Blessed be His name, and His mention
shall be exalted for ever and ever.[2]

If we compare these principles with the Shema we
find that they add the belief that the God of Israel is
the transcendent and omniscient creator of all things,
and also a belief in the coming of the Messiah (the
descendant of King David who will institute God's
perfect rule of peace and justice over the world) and a
belief in the bodily resurrection ('revival') of the dead.

Historically, these principles have achieved near
universal acceptance within Judaism, and they remain
a good summary of generally accepted Jewish beliefs
to this day. If we look at the three main movements
in contemporary Judaism, Orthodox Judaism would
accept all of them, Conservative Judaism would also
accept all of them while allowing a place for modern
critical ideas about the historical origins of the Jewish
law, and Reformed Judaism would accept the first
five while arguing that there needs to be flexibility
as to what parts of the law need to be obeyed today
and rejecting belief in the coming of a Messiah and in
bodily resurrection.

In terms of human flourishing, Judaism would say
that human flourishing for those who are Jews
means living in obedience to God by observing the
commandments of God set out in the Torah. By living

2 From David Birnbaum, *Jews, Church & Civilization* Volume
III (Millennium Education Foundation, 2005), 157.

in this way, they are able to flourish in this world (see Psalm 1:1–3) and will have a place in God's kingdom in the world to come. For those who are not Jews, the Jewish tradition has traditionally said that for non-Jews, flourishing means observance of what are known as the Noachide laws, a set of universal moral laws given by God as a covenant with Noah and with the 'sons of Noah' – that is, all of humanity (see Genesis 9:1–18).

In the words of the Jewish Virtual Library:

> The Noachide laws are seven laws considered by rabbinic tradition as the minimal moral duties required by the Bible on all men. While Jews are obligated to observe the whole Torah – 613 commandments, every non-Jew is considered a 'son of the covenant of Noah' and he who accepts these obligations is considered a righteous person who is guaranteed a place in the world to come.
>
> The seven Noachide laws, as traditionally enumerated are:

1. Do Not Deny God

2. Do Not Blaspheme God

3. Do Not Murder

4. Do Not Engage in Incestuous, Adulterous or Homosexual Relationships

5. Do Not Steal

6. Do Not Eat of a Live Animal

7. Establish Courts/Legal System to Ensure Law Obedience

    Except for the seventh law, all are negative commands, and the last itself is usually interpreted as commanding the enforcement of the others. They are derived exegetically from divine demands addressed to Adam and Noah, the progenitors of all mankind, and are thus regarded as universal.[3]

Christianity and the Jewish universe

Christians accept the worldview set out in the Shema and in the thirteen principles of Maimonides. However, they want to add to them.

First, they want to say that the one creator God is the Triune God who is Father, Son and Holy Spirit.

Secondly, they want to say that God has fulfilled his promise to send the Messiah by becoming incarnate in the person of Jesus Christ (the word 'Christ' means 'Messiah'). This means that whereas the twelfth principle of Maimonides looks for the first coming of the Messiah, Christians look for his coming again in glory to judge the living and the dead and to bring in God's new creation.

---

3 Jewish Virtual Library, 'Jewish Concepts: The Seven Noahide Laws' at https://www.jewishvirtuallibrary.org/the-seven-noachide-laws.

Thirdly, they want to say that in his death Jesus took upon himself the judgement that all human beings deserve for their failure to obey God's law, that his resurrection broke the power of death and will lead in due time to the resurrection of all other human beings, and that his gift of the Holy Spirit enables believers to live a new life lived marked by obedience to God and a new relationship with God in which they can call him 'Abba! Father!' (Galatians 4:6).

Fourthly, they want to say that by his death and resurrection Jesus has inaugurated a renewed Israel consisting of both Jews and Gentiles on an equal footing and that in this new Israel, while the moral law of God still needs to be obeyed, the sacrificial and ritual laws given by God to Old Testament Israel are no longer obligatory.

Two further differences between Christianity and Judaism which need to be noted concern the biblical canon and the theological status of the land of Israel.

Concerning the biblical canon, Christians add the twenty-seven new books of the New Testament to the thirty-nine books contained in the Hebrew Bible (what they would call the 'Old Testament'). These books contain the witness of the Jesus' apostles to how he has fulfilled and will fulfil the promises made by God in the Hebrew Bible (see Luke 24:44–49).

Concerning the status of the land of Israel, many Jews would continue to say that God's promise of the land of Israel to the people of Israel (Genesis 15:18–21) remains in force, and that within Israel the Temple Mount, the site of the Jewish temple, is the place where God's presence is manifested more than anywhere else on earth (which is why Jews turn towards it when they pray and why they insert written prayers into the cracks in the Western wall of the Temple Mount).

There are Christian Zionists who would agree with these beliefs, but the mainstream Christian position is that, since the coming of Jesus, the whole world has become equally the land of promise and the place where God dwells on earth is in the hearts of believers through his Spirit rather than the Temple in Jerusalem. However, this does not mean that the land was not promised by God to the Jewish people, nor does it deny the moral right of Jewish people to live there today.

Judaism and Christianity on human flourishing

As we have seen, Judaism understands human flourishing in terms of Jewish obedience to the Torah and Gentile obedience to the Noachide laws. Christianity by contrast sees human flourishing as God's gift of new life given through the Spirit to all those (whether Jew or Gentile) who believe in Jesus and are baptised. This new life does involve obedience to God's law, but this obedience is the fruit of the new life given by the Spirit. It is the outworking of a new relationship with God rather than its cause (see Romans 6:1–14, 8:1–17).

"Christianity by contrast sees human flourishing as God's gift of new life given through the Spirit to all those (whether Jew or Gentile) who believe in Jesus and are baptised."

Christian
Jewish Islamic
multiverse
postmodern
materialist
Living
well
deist
Hindu
Sik

6. The Islamic Universe

Islam is the second largest religion in the world after Christianity with some 1.8 billion adherents worldwide. It began in Arabia in the seventh century as a monotheistic movement led by Muhammad which challenged the prevailing Arabian polytheism.

There are two major branches of Islam – the majority Sunni community (85–90% of Muslims) and the minority Shia community (10–15% of Muslims). The division between them originated in the seventh century in differences about who should succeed Muhammad as the leader (caliph) of Islam. Each branch has different groups within it (such as, for instance, the Salafist reform movement within Sunni Islam that is dominant in Saudi Arabia), and in both branches there is a debate about how traditional Islamic teaching and practice relate to today's world.

All this, plus the many different cultures and backgrounds from which Muslims come, means that there is great diversity in Islam, as there is in Christianity and Judaism. Nevertheless, it still possible to talk about an overall Islamic worldview.

The foundation for the Islamic worldview is the basic creed of Islam, the Shahadah, which Muslims are under an obligation to recite daily. In English translation this creed states, 'There is no god but God. Muhammad is the messenger of God.' The first half emphasises the oneness of God over against polytheism, and the second emphasises the role played by Muhammad as God's final messenger to humankind.

Expanding these two points, we can summarise the overall Islamic worldview as follows:

First, Muslims believe in one wholly transcendent God (in Arabic, *Allah*) who has no offspring, no race, no sex and no body, and is unaffected by the characteristics of human life. This one God created all things, the material universe, the angels who worship God and carry out God's orders throughout the universe, and the human race. Furthermore, everything that happens is governed by God's decrees (hence the commonly used Arabic expression, '*inshallah*', 'if God wills it').

Secondly, human beings are rational creatures created by God to live in obedience to him and to rule as his vice-gerents over the world. However, as is shown by the Islamic version of the story of Adam and Eve, human beings have been created by God as weak, fallible and forgetful beings and therefore easily led astray from obedience to God.

Thirdly, to counteract this human tendency to stray from obedience to God and to worship other gods instead of him, God has sent a series of messengers or 'prophets' to the nations of the world to remind human beings who they ought to worship and how they ought to live. The first prophet was Adam and other prophets include Noah, Abraham, Moses, David and Jesus. The last and most important of these prophets was Muhammad, who was sent by God to bring the message of Islam to all humankind.

Fourthly, God revealed holy books or scriptures to a number of these prophets. These include the Scrolls (given to Abraham), the Torah (given to Moses), the

Psalms (given to David), the Gospel (given to Jesus) and the Quran (given to Muhammad).[1] In their original form all these writings contained the same identical message, but the other writings have been corrupted by Jews and Christians, and only the Quran in Arabic contains exactly the words revealed by God.

Fifthly, there are two key sources of instruction for those who want to live according to God's will. The first is the Quran, which is divided into 114 *suras* or chapters, which are in turn divided into *ayats* or verses. The second is the Sunnah, the tradition of the words and deeds of the Muhammad. Muhammad is considered by Muslims to have perfectly exemplified what it means to live rightly before God and so the Sunnah as well as the Quran tells Muslims how they too ought to live. Sharia, the tradition of Islamic jurisprudence, reflects what generations of Islamic scholars have taught about how Muslims should live, individually and communally, in accordance with the Quran and the Sunnah.[2]

Sixthly, at the end of time there will be a day of judgement in which human beings will be judged for their actions in this life. Those people who have followed God's guidance will be rewarded with a place in heaven (described in the Quran as 'gardens of perpetual bliss') and those people who have rejected God's guidance will be punished with hell, a place of perpetual torment.

---

1 The Arabic original is also often transliterated into English as *Koran*.
2 For an English translation of the Quran, see N. J. Darwood, *The Koran* (London: Penguin Classics, 2014). For an English translation of the Sunnah see https://sunnah.com/.

Alongside this worldview, and giving expression to it, are five forms of Islamic practice (the 'five pillars of Islam') which need to be observed by all Muslims who are capable of doing so. These are, the recitation of the Shahadah, observing the five daily times of prayer, performing acts of charity, fasting during the Islamic holy month of Ramadan, and undertaking at least one pilgrimage to Mecca. In the Quran and subsequent Islamic tradition each of these pillars carries with it promises of reward, blessing and paradise.

What all this means is that in the Islamic universe to flourish as a human being involves living in obedience to God's will in accordance with the instructions given in the Quran and the Sunnah, which in turn means observing the five pillars of Islam if it is possible to do so. Those who live in this way flourish in this world and can hope to flourish in paradise forever after they die.

Christianity and the Islamic universe

At first sight it might appear that Muslims and Christians share a very similar worldview. Like Muslims, Christians believe:

- There is one transcendent, personal, God who has created and who rules over all things.

- God has created human beings as rational creatures who are called to live in obedience to him and to rule as vice-gerents over his creation.

- God has communicated his will to his human creatures through messengers whom he has appointed (one of whom was Jesus), and he has preserved their messages in a series of holy writings.

- God will judge all human beings at the end of time, resulting in some people going to heaven and others going to hell.

However, these apparent agreements between the Islamic and Christian worldviews conceal fundamental differences between the worldviews of the two religions. Muslims and Christians share many words, but the meanings they give to these words is very different.

First, Islam specifically rejects the basic Christian conviction that God is the Trinity of Father, Son and Holy Spirit and that God the Son became incarnate in the person of the God–Man Jesus Christ. Thus, addressing Christians (the 'people of the book'), the Quran states:

> O people of the Book! Commit no excesses in your religion: nor say of Allah aught but truth. Christ Jesus the son of Mary was (no more than) an Apostle of Allah and His Word which He bestowed on Mary and a Spirit proceeding from Him: so believe in Allah and his Apostles. Say not 'Trinity': desist: it will be better for you: for Allah is One Allah: glory be to him: (for Exalted is He) above having a son. To him belong all things in heaven

and on earth. And enough is Allah as a
Disposer of affairs. (Surah 4:171)

For Islam, Jesus was a prophet reiterating previous
declarations of God's will and pointing forward to the
coming of Muhammad.

Secondly, while affirming Jesus' virgin birth, Islam
denies Jesus' death on the cross and subsequent
resurrection, holding that God took Jesus directly to
paradise and substituted someone else in his place.
Thus, the Quran declares concerning the Jews:

> That they said (in boast) 'We killed Jesus
> the son of Mary the Apostle of Allah; but
> they killed him not nor crucified him but
> so it was made to appear to them and
> those who differ therein are full of doubts
> with no (certain) knowledge but only a
> conjecture to follow for of a surety they
> killed him not.

> Nay, Allah raised him up unto Himself;
> and Allah is exalted in Power Wise.'
> (Surah 4:157)

Thirdly, Islam and Christianity differ over the human
plight and its solution. As the Christian writer on
Islam, Andy Bannister, explains:

> ...for the Qu'ran the problem is human
> ignorance and forgetfulness; the solution
> is knowledge and information. By
> contrast, for the Bible, the problem is our
> sinful nature and alienation from God; the

solution is atonement and reconciliation.[3]

Furthermore, as we saw in chapter 1, for Christianity atonement and reconciliation are possible because the Triune God took human nature upon himself at the incarnation, in the person of the God–Man Jesus Christ, died and rose to give the human race a fresh start through the defeat of sin and death, and makes this fresh start effective through the work of the Holy Spirit, who makes those who believe the holy children of God and enables them to call God Father (Romans 8:1–17, Galatians 4:1–7).

These are all beliefs which the Quran denies, and this brings us to the final issue between Christianity and Islam. Islam claims that the Quran, given by God himself, teaches what is also taught in the holy books that preceded the Quran, what Christians call the Old and New Testaments. However, as Christians see it, study of the Old and New Testaments shows that they teach the beliefs held by Christianity, which are different from the beliefs taught by the Quran.

Islamic scholars attempt to get round this issue in two ways. Either they argue that there has been major textual corruption in the present versions of the Old and New Testaments (something for which there is no evidence), or that Christian theology has misunderstood and/or misrepresented the message of the Old and New Testaments (something which the Quran itself seems to maintain, in passages such as Surah 4:47 and 5:15–16, but for which again there is no evidence).

---

3 Andy Bannister, *Do Muslims and Christians Worship the Same God?* (London: Inter-Varsity Press, 2021), 95.

This is a major problem for Islam, because it means that either the Quran is wrong in maintaining that the Old and New Testaments were inspired by God, or that the Quran is wrong in what it teaches about God and his saving activity. Either way, the basic claim of Islam, namely, that the Quran revealed by God to Muhammad gives a truthful account of God and his activity, is mistaken.

From a Christian perspective this means that in the end the claims made by Islam contradict each other. Christianity agrees with Islam that the books of the Old and New Testaments were inspired by God, but that for precisely this reason Islamic theology is mistaken in what it says about God, the human plight and God's solution to it.

Islam and Christianity on human flourishing

In Islam, as we have noted, human flourishing involves living in obedience to the will of God made known through the Quran and the Sunnah. By contrast, as we saw when comparing Jewish and Christian views of human flourishing, Christianity sees human flourishing as God's gift of new life given through the Spirit to all those who believe in Jesus and are baptised. This new life involves obedience to God's will, but (a) in Christianity, the shape of such obedience is made known through the Bible rather than the Quran and the Sunnah; and (b) in Christianity such obedience is the fruit of the new relationship with God given through the Holy Spirit rather than something people have to achieve in their own strength.

"Christianity sees human
flourishing as God's gift
of new life given through
the Spirit to all those
who believe in Jesus and are
baptised."

Christian
Jewish Islamic
multiverse
postmodern
materialist
Living
well
deist
Hindu

7. The Hindu Universe

Hinduism is the world's third largest religious tradition after Christianity and Islam, with some 1.2 billion adherents.

The centre of Hinduism remains India, where the majority of the population are Hindu, where Hinduism is extremely significant culturally and where Hindu nationalism is now a very important political force. However, as a result of emigration there are now Hindu communities across the world. For example, there is now a very large Hindu temple – the Shri Swaminarayan Mandir – in Neasden in north-west London. Interest in Hinduism as an alternative worldview to either Christianity or materialism has grown across the Western world since the nineteenth century, and there a number of practices which have become prevalent in modern Western culture that are Hindu in origin, such as yoga and the practice of mindfulness.

Hinduism is not something that is easy to define. It is a form of religion that has gradually developed in South Asia over many thousands of years and that encompasses a vast range of religious beliefs and practices. Nevertheless, in spite of Hinduism's immense diversity, there are a set of texts which can be said to form the Hindu scriptures and which provide the basis for Hindu religious activity.

The most important of these texts are the Vedas. These are the fundamental texts of Hinduism and are viewed as containing eternal truths revealed to the ancient sages by Brahman (the supreme reality underlying all things). There are four Vedas: the Rigveda, the Samaveda, the Yajurveda and the Atharavaveda. Each of these four Vedas has been sub-classified into four major types of text: the Samhitas (mantras and benedictions), the Aranyakas (texts on rituals, ceremonies, sacrifices and symbolic sacrifices), the Brahmanas (commentaries on rituals, ceremonies and sacrifices), and the Upanishads (texts discussing meditation, philosophy and spiritual knowledge).

Alongside the Vedas, and regarded as compatible with them, there are a variety of other texts which have helped to shape Hindu belief and practice. These include epic texts such as the Mahabharata and the Ramayana, the Puranas, an encyclopaedic collection of texts on a diverse range of topics including cosmogony, cosmology, the genealogies of the gods, goddesses, demigods, kings, heroes and sages, folk tales, pilgrimages, temples, medicine, astronomy, grammar, mineralogy, humour and love stories, as well as theology and philosophy, and legal texts such as the Law of Manu, which has traditionally been regarded as the basis for the Hindu caste system. Part of the Mahabharata is the Bhagavad Gita, a text which is sometimes regarded as an additional Upanishad because its contents are seen as similar to the Upanishads in the Vedas.[1]

Based on these texts and others, there is an overall Hindu worldview which views the existence of both the cosmos as whole, and of particular human beings

[1] For an English translation of the texts mentioned in these two paragraphs see R. C. Zaehner, *Hindu Scriptures* (London and New York: Everyman, 1992).

within it, in cyclical terms. The cosmos (made up of numerous universes) has been created and destroyed numerous times in a process, known as the *kalpa* cycle, that will go on forever. This cycle of creation and destruction is without any purpose. It is simply what is described as a form of 'play' (*lila*) by Brahman, the supreme reality underlying the cosmos.

Human existence consists of a cycle of birth, death and rebirth in which the non-material soul (*atman*) passes through various forms of reincarnation (*samsara*) which may be in a human or non-human form. The nature of these reincarnations depends on how the previous life was lived, in line with the principle of *karma*, the principle that all actions have consequences either in this life or in the next.

In order to live well in each successive incarnation, one needs to behave in accordance with *dharma*, the order which governs the cosmos and human behaviour within it. The more one lives in accordance with *dharma* in this life, the better one's next reincarnation will be. The Hindu caste system has traditionally been based on this idea. Thus, one person is a high caste Brahmin because they have lived well according to *dharma* in their previous life while another person is a low-class Shudra because they have lived less well. The eventual goal of human existence is to achieve *moksha*, liberation from this whole cycle of death and rebirth.

As has already been noted, a vast variety of different forms of belief and practice have developed on the basis of these texts and this basic worldview. For example, the majority of Hindus are theists, while the Samkhya school of Hinduism is atheistic. However, there are two forms of Hinduism that are most likely to be encountered by people living in the UK. These are Vedanta Hinduism and Bhakti Hinduism.

Vedanta Hinduism is a form of Hindu philosophy which developed in the sixth century BC and which draws its inspiration from the teaching contained in the Upanishads. In this form of Hinduism, Brahman is beyond all thought, reason, and conceptualisation. Thus, the Chandokya Upanishad describes learning about Brahman as receiving: 'that instruction by which we hear what cannot be heard, by which we perceive what cannot be perceived, by which we know what cannot be known.'[2] Because this supreme reality is beyond description, we cannot describe it as being personal, but what we can say is that this supreme reality is the only thing that truly exists and therefore anything else that appears to exist is *maya*, or illusion. To quote James Sire, for Vedanta Hinduism:

> ...anything that appears to exist as a separate and distinct object – this chair, not that one; this rock, not that tree; me, not you – is an illusion. It is not our separateness that gives us reality, it is our oneness, that fact that we are Brahman and Brahman is one. Yes, Brahman is *the* One.[3]

In the Vedanta tradition, the way to achieve *moksha* is to experience the truth that 'Atman is Brahman' that Brahman and the soul are identical. This state

---

2 Chandokya Upanishad, Chapter 6, Khanda 1 at https://sacred-texts.com/hin/sbe01119.htm.
3 Sire, *Universe Next Door*, 139 (italics in the original).

is achieved through a life of dedicated meditation and the Mandukya Upanishad refers to it as the 'awakened life of pure consciousness.' Paradoxically, this 'life of pure consciousness' is one in which there is no consciousness of anything at all. This is because such consciousness would involve a dualism between knower and known, rather than the state where *moksha* is achieved because everything is experienced as one.

By contrast, Bhakti (or devotional) Hinduism is a form of Hinduism which involves devotion to the Hindu gods Vishnu, Shiva, or Kali, or one of their many incarnations or avatars, such as Krishna, the incarnation of Vishnu. In the words of Winfried Corduan:

> This is the religion of the majority of Hindus. Many of them have never even heard of the Atman–Brahman identity and for many of those who have, it is a piece of speculation that is not very relevant to them. They worship personal gods, who are ultimately without form, but who – for our sake – have taken abode in the statues in temples so that people can have an easy opportunity to worship them.[4]

The purpose of the worship of these gods is to achieve *moksha*. Thus, in the Bhagavad Gita Krishna declares: 'After attaining Me, the great souls do not incur rebirth in this miserable transitory world, because

_____
4 Winfried Corduan, 'Hinduism' in Winfried Corduan et al, 'Eastern Religions', *Areopagus Journal* 9:3 (2009), Loc. 307.

they have attained the highest perfection.'

However, as Corduan goes on to explain, we should not, 'think of this offer as free grace. For the most part devotion to a god implies a life of complete dedication, which it is not easy to carry out.'[5] For instance, in the Bhagavad Gita the hero Arjuna is told: 'Fly unto Him [Krishna] alone for refuge with your whole being, Arjuna. From His grace, you shall attain supreme peace and the eternal abode.' What this involves is Arjuna practising the yoga, or form of life, that Krishna commands and focusing his entire being on Krishna, all day and every day. The offer is one of deliverance through complete obedience.

Although, as we have noted, there are numerous different forms of Hinduism, what they all have in common is that they all hold that to flourish as a human being means to live in way that will enable you to eventually attain *moksha*, escape from the cycle of death and rebirth.

Christianity and the Hindu universe

Christians agree with Hindus that there is a supreme reality underlying all things, that the world is governed by an objective moral order, and that how one behaves in relation to this moral order has consequences not only for this life, but for the life to come. However, there are also fundamental differences between Christianity and Hinduism.

5 Corduan, 'Hinduism', Loc. 335.

"Rather than saying that there is an endless and purposeless cycle of creation and destruction, it teaches that God created all things for a purpose and that that purpose will be fully and eternally fulfilled."

Christian
Jewish Islamic
multiverse
postmodern
materialist
Living
well
deist
Hindu
Sik

First, the Christian belief in God as the supreme reality means that Christians disagree with the atheism of the Samkhya school of Hinduism in the same way and for the same reasons that they disagree with the materialist atheism that exists in Western thought.

Secondly, the Christian doctrine of creation rules out the cosmic pessimism of the *kalpa* cycle. Rather than saying that there is an endless and purposeless cycle of creation and destruction, it teaches that God created all things for a purpose and that that purpose will be fully and eternally fulfilled.

Thirdly, the Christian doctrine of creation also rules out the Hindu belief in reincarnation. This is because Christianity holds that each person is created by God as a unique being consisting as a material body and an immaterial soul united together and so it makes no sense to say that that person can exist in some other bodily form. It is because humans are a combination of body and soul that the Christian hope for the future is a resurrection life involving both, a hope that is based on the resurrection in body and soul of Jesus Christ.

Fourthly, the Christian doctrine of creation further rules out the Hindu idea of *karma*. If I have not lived a former life, then the conditions of my life in this world cannot be the result of what I did in that former life. In addition, belief in *karma* also logically entails the conviction that there is no value in relieving the sufferings of others since they need to experience those sufferings as the necessary outworking of their previous misdeeds.

Fifthly, from a Christian perspective the view of the Vedanta tradition that the purpose of existence is to learn the truth that 'Atman is Brahman' – that I am the infinite God – makes no sense. If the infinite is truly infinite then it must know it is infinite (otherwise it would not be infinite in knowledge). Hence the person seeking to know that they are infinite cannot truly be infinite. What is more, the pantheism of the Vedanta tradition logically involves the annihilation of the distinction between good and evil. If everything is one, then so are good and evil.

Finally, from a Christian perspective, the worship of the gods in the Bhakti tradition of Hinduism is a form of the age-old human tendency to idolatry. Like the gods of Greek and Roman mythology which the early Christians refused to worship, the Hindu gods do not truly exist. They are human constructs and the worship of them violates the command to worship God alone (Exodus 20:3–4). Furthermore, their non-existence means that any help one may think they can offer is illusory. Only the 'living and true God' (1 Thessalonians 1:9), the 'unknown God' (Acts 17:23–24) whom Hindus are unconsciously seeking can give them the *moksha* that they desire.

Hinduism and Christianity on human flourishing

As we have noted, for Hinduism human flourishing is about escaping from the *kalpa* cycle of death and rebirth. The various forms of Hinduism are different forms of spiritual discipline intended to enable people to achieve this end. For Christianity by contrast, the cycle of numerous deaths and rebirths does not exist. Humans have one life to live which will result in either eternal happiness with God or eternal misery in separation from him.

Furthermore, in Hinduism the achievement of *moksha* is in the last resort something that human beings have to do for themselves. In Christianity by contrast, eternal life with God, starting in this world and reaching its ultimate fulfilment in the world to come is a free gift from God (Romans 6:23) to all those who through God's grace believe in Jesus and are baptised.

8. The Buddhist Universe

Buddhism is the world's fourth largest religion, with over 520 million followers. It traces its origins to the teaching and practice of the Buddha, Siddhartha Gautama, who lived sometime in the sixth century BC.

He was born into a royal family in present-day Nepal and lived a life of privilege and luxury until one day he left the royal enclosure and encountered for the first time an old man, a sick man, a corpse, and lastly an ascetic holy man who was apparently content and at peace with the world. As a result of these four encounters, he abandoned royal life and entered on a spiritual quest that eventually led him to become enlightened (the term Buddha means 'enlightened one') about how to escape from being trapped in the endless cycle of suffering and reincarnation. Following this enlightenment, he attracted a band of followers, instituted a monastic order and spent the rest of his life travelling throughout the north-eastern part of the Indian subcontinent teaching others about the path of awakening that he had discovered.

There are now numerous schools of Buddhism that seek to follow the path laid down by the Buddha in a variety of different ways. The two largest are Theravada Buddhism, which is most popular in Sri Lanka, Cambodia, Thailand, Laos and Myanmar, and Mahayana Buddhism, which is strongest in Tibet, China, Taiwan, Japan, Korea and Mongolia. Although Buddhism is strongest in South and Southeast Asia, as in the case of Hinduism there are now Buddhist communities around the world.

For most Buddhists, the foundations of their belief and practice lie in what are known as the 'three jewels'. These are the Buddha himself, the teachings of Buddha (the Dharma) and the congregations of monastic practitioners (the Sangha) who preserve the authentic teachings of the Buddha and provide further examples of the truth of the Buddha's teaching that enlightenment is attainable. There is no one single text that is regarded as spiritually authoritative by all Buddhists with the Theravada and Mahayana schools of Buddhism each having their own set of texts (the Pali Canon and Mahayana Sutras respectively).[1]

In spite of the diversity within Buddhism, it is possible to talk about an overall Buddhist worldview. In this worldview, although there are a variety of spiritual beings who in Western terms would be described as gods and demons, there is no creator God, rather the universe is simply the working out of a cyclical process in which world-systems come into being, exist for a time, are destroyed and are then re-made. Within this cyclical worldview, human beings are also seen as being trapped in an endless process of reincarnation, experiencing suffering through many lives on the basis of their behaviour in previous incarnations (what is known as 'contingent origination'). Only achieving *nirvana*, or liberation, through enlightenment can lead to freedom from this cycle of death and rebirth.

The account of the Buddhist view of being human outlined in the last two sentences of the previous paragraph might seem to suggest the Buddhists believe, in accordance with Hindu and Western

1 For an English translation of key Buddhist texts, see Donald Lopez, *Buddhist Scriptures* (London: Penguin, 2004).

thought, that there are persons who are trapped in the cycle of reincarnation and who require liberation through enlightenment. There are Buddhists today who present such a 'personalist' account of Buddhist anthropology, but this is not the mainstream Buddhist way of looking at the matter. The mainstream Buddhist view is the 'no soul' view of humanity.

The no soul view holds that what we normally think of as persons are a bundle of different elements that only momentarily exist, and that what we think of as the enduring existence of persons over time is simply a sequence of such bundles one after the other. This point is made by the Buddha in the Potthapada Sutta as follows:

> Kitta, the son of an elephant trainer, inquired of the Enlightened One (the Buddha) whether any of the three modes of personality – the past you, the present you, and the future you – are real.

> The Enlightened One replied:

> Just so, Kitta, as from a cow comes milk, and from the milk curds, and from the curds butter, and from the butter ghee, and from the ghee junket; but when it is milk it is not called curds, or butter, or ghee or junket; and when it is curds it is not called by any of the other names and so on. Just so, Kitta when any of the three modes of personality is going on, it is not called by the name of the other. For these, Kitta, are merely names, expressions, terms of speech, designations in

common use in the world. And of these,
a Tahthagata (one who has won the truth)
makes use, but is not led astray by them.

The point here is that just as milk, curds, butter, ghee
and junket are different things that exist in sequence,
so it is with the past, present and future selves. We
should not be led astray by the common use of
the term 'you' to think that there is a continuously
existing self in the past, present and future. This
understanding that there is no self, what is known as
anatta, is a key part of the 'four noble truths,' the four
key elements of the Buddha's teaching.

As Peter Kreeft explains:

> The first noble truth is that all of life is
> *dukkha*, suffering. The word means out-
> of-joint-ness or separation – something
> similar to sin but without the personal
> relational dimension: not a broken
> relationship but a broken consciousness.
> Inner brokenness is Buddhism's 'bad
> news,' which precedes its gospel, or
> 'good news.'

> The second noble truth is that the cause of
> suffering is *tanha*, grasping selfish desire.
> We suffer because of the gap between
> what we want and what we have. This
> gap is created by our dissatisfaction, our
> wanting to get what we do not have or
> wanting to keep what we do have (e.g.,
> life, which causes fear of death). Thus
> desire is the villain for Buddha, the cause
> of all suffering.

This [second truth] explains the no-soul doctrine. Desire creates the illusion of a desirer alienated from the desired object, the illusion of twoness. Enlightenment is the extinction of this illusion. 'I want that' creates the illusion of an 'I' distinct from the 'that'; and this distinction is the cause of suffering. Desire is thus the fuel of suffering's fire.

The third noble truth follows inevitably. To remove the cause is to remove the effect, therefore suffering can be extinguished (*nirvana*) by extinguishing its cause, desire. Remove the fuel and you put out the fire.

The fourth noble truth tells you how to extinguish desire: by the 'noble eightfold path' of ego reduction in each of life's eight defined areas, inward and outward (e.g., right thought, right associations).[2]

The 'eightfold path' consists of:

1. Right understanding (the acceptance of Buddhist teachings)

2. Right intention (a commitment to cultivate right attitudes)

3. Right speech (truthful speech that avoids slander, gossip and abuse)

2 Peter Kreeft, *Fundamentals of the Faith* (San Francisco: Ignatius Press, 1988), 99–100.

4. Right action (engaging in peaceful and harmonious behaviour, and refraining from stealing, killing and overindulgence in sensual pleasure)

5. Right livelihood (avoiding making a living in harmful ways such as exploiting people, killing animals or trading in intoxicants or weapons)

6. Right effort (freeing oneself from evil and unwholesome states of mind and preventing them from arising in future)

7. Right mindfulness (developing an awareness of the body, sensations, feelings and states of mind)

8. Right concentration (the development of the mental focus necessary for this awareness)

At the basis of Buddhist ethics are what are known as the 'five lay precepts' which are not absolute commands or prohibitions, but training rules designed to enable people to live a life in which they are happy, without worries, and can meditate well. These five precepts are not to kill, steal, lie, commit sexual misconduct or take intoxicants.

These five basic precepts are expanded to eight for lay people who want to adopt an ascetic way of life, to ten for novice monks and nuns, and to more detailed sets of rules for those who have fully embraced a monastic way of life (227 rules in the Theravada tradition). All these precepts and rules are intended to help people travel the path to *nirvana* more effectively.

In Buddhism, as in Hinduism, human flourishing means escaping from the cycle of death and rebirth. Doing this (achieving *nirvana*) involves overcoming the illusion of the separate existence of the self by extinguishing the desire that is the cause of this illusion. The noble eightfold path is the way that leads to the extinguishing of desire and the other precepts and rules in the Buddhist tradition are designed to help people travel this way.

Christianity and the Buddhist universe

Christians agree with Buddhism that the untamed desires of the ego are a serious problem for human beings since they are what prevent us from living rightly before God (see Genesis 3:1–7). They also agree with many, if not all, of the forms of behaviour contained in the eightfold path and the five lay precepts.

However, from a Christian perspective there are also four major problems with the Buddhist worldview.

First, the non-theistic nature of Buddhist cosmology is unsatisfactory because it runs into the same problem as the Western rejection of God's existence – namely, that the existence of an absolute, intelligent, personal and wholly good creator God is the only satisfactory explanation of the world in which we live. In addition, Christians also would question the existence of the deities that are acknowledged in Buddhism and would see the worship given to them in some forms of Buddhism as a form of idolatry.

Secondly, the Buddhist teaching of an endless cosmic cycle of creation and destruction and its belief in reincarnation raise the same problems as the Hindu version of the same ideas noted in the last chapter.

Thirdly, the Buddhist 'no soul' doctrine not only goes against the Christian belief that each individual self does exist and will continue to exist because of the activity of God in creating, preserving and resurrecting them, but is also internally incoherent. As Keith Yandell notes, in Buddhist thought:

> Enlightenment occurs when full acceptance of the typical Buddhist doctrine of what lies behind talk of a self is joined by bliss, peace and detachment. In a meditative state, you 'see' the structure of your existence as nothing more than a collection of states.[3]

The problem for Buddhists is that analysis of this statement reveals that, for it to be true, the collection of states that is enlightened has to be a collection of states that has one overall experience, is aware of having this experience, and that can act because it can recall the past and look forward to the future. What is that if it is not a 'self'? Ultimately Buddhists are in the self-refuting position of the man who cries, 'I do not exist.'

What is more, there is no reason to think that this self does not continue to exist over an extended period of time, rather than simply at one moment.

---

3 Keith Yandell, 'Buddhism,' in Corduan et al, 'Eastern Religions', Loc. 460.

The fourth and final problem lies in Buddhism's blanket rejection of desire. To quote Kreeft again, on this issue:

> Christianity and Buddhism seem about as far apart as possible. For where Buddha finds our desires too strong, Christ finds them too weak. [Christ] wants us to love more, not less: to love God with our whole heart, soul, mind, and strength. Buddha "solves" the problem of pain by a spiritual euthanasia: curing the disease of egotism and the suffering it brings by killing the patient, the ego, self, soul, or I–image of God (I AM) in man.[4]

However, as he goes on to say:

> ...perhaps things are not quite as contradictory as that. For the desire Buddha speaks of is only selfish desire. He does not distinguish unselfish love (*agape*) from selfish love (*eros*); he simply does not know of *agape* at all. He profoundly knows and condemns the desire to possess something less than ourselves, like money, sex, or power; but he does not know the desire to be possessed by something more than ourselves. Buddha knows greed, but not God. And surely we Westerners, whose lives and economic systems are often based on greed, need to hear Buddha when he speaks about what he knows and we have forgotten.

4 Kreeft, *Fundamentals of the Faith*, 100.

But Buddhists even more desperately need to hear what they do not know: the good news about God and his love.[5]

Buddhism and Christianity on human flourishing

As we have seen, for Buddhism human flourishing involves overcoming the desire that causes the illusion of a separate self and thus keeps one trapped in the cycle of death and rebirth. For Christianity, by contrast, the created self is not an illusion but a reality and the problem that human beings face is not the existence of desire, but the desire for the wrong things. Thus, from a Christian perspective it is a sin to desire one's neighbour's wife, or house or livestock (Exodus 20:17), but it is virtuous to desire the glorification of God's name or one's neighbour's well-being.

It follows that for Christianity human flourishing means not the extinction of the illusion of the self through the extinction of desire, but the creation of selves who have right desires, selves that say, 'I delight to do your will, O my God' (Psalm 40:8). The purpose of the saving action of God in Jesus Christ and through the Holy Spirit is to bring about human flourishing through the creation of such selves.

---

5 Kreeft, *Fundamentals of the Faith*, 100.

"For Christianity, by contrast, the created self is not an illusion but a reality and the problem that human beings face is not the existence of desire, but the desire for the wrong things."

Christian Jewish Islamic multiverse postmodern materialist Living well deist Hindu Sik

9. The Sikh Universe

Sikhism is the youngest and fifth largest of the world's major religions. There are approximately twenty million Sikhs in the world, the majority of whom live in the province of Punjab in north-west India, although there is now a worldwide Sikh diaspora (for example, there is a large Sikh temple, the Guru Nanak Darbar Gurdwara, in Gravesend in Kent).

Sikhism began to develop in the fifteenth century in the Punjab district of what are now India and Pakistan (the district was divided between the two at the Partition of India in 1947). It was founded by Guru Nanak (1469–1539) and is based on his teachings and that of the nine gurus who followed him.

The fundamental tenet of Sikhs is belief in the *Ik Onkar*, the 'one constant', which in Western terms translates into belief in one God who creates and sustains all things. What Sikhs believe about God is set out in the opening line of the Sikh scriptures, the Adi Granth. This declares:

> There is but one all-pervading spirit, and
> truth is its name! It exists in all creation;
> it does not fear; it does not hate; it is
> timeless and universal and self-existent.

All human beings, regardless of sex, race or religion, are the creation of this one God and as such have equal value and dignity. Like Hinduism and Buddhism, Sikhism believes that human beings exist within a cosmic cycle of life, death and rebirth. All beings, animal and human, have within them a soul, or *atma*, which is a part of God. The form of existence that each soul has in each new life depends on the operation of the law of *karma* which determines the form of that life in accordance with how the soul behaved in its previous life.

Once again like Hinduism and Buddhism, the central question to which Sikhism provides an answer is how to escape from this cycle in which it takes 8.4 million reincarnations for a soul to be born as human being. The answer that Sikhism provides is that the way of escape (called *mukti* or liberation) is through achieving total knowledge of, and union with, God. In order to achieve *mukti* a person has to switch the focus of their attention from themselves to God and live accordingly. This is something that happens through the grace of God at work in a person and takes place as God shows them the way to attain union with him through their own personal religious experience, and through the teaching of holy books and holy people. To quote the Adi Granth again:

> The man who is lost in selfishness is drowned without water, his mind is like a fog and his vice like mud. Yet the Lord is the ocean and the disciple a little fish; once this is realised, a union becomes possible, and that is like metal being welded to metal, like water mixing with water. This union is achieved by the word of the true Guru. Man's heart is penetrated by the Guru's word, it is imperishable and has the power to create and to destroy. Once it comes it is as though a lotus flower blossoms in the heart; it serves as a ship whereby we may

cross the evil ocean of existence. The one who is asleep is awakened, and he who was aflame with fever is cooled. Once this experience comes no one will assert that he has deserved it. It is as though the disciple has no purity of its own, but the Lord seizes his arm and washes him. Then the body ceases to be a puppet of maya and is free to serve the true Guru.

The way of life that Sikhs see as forming the path to liberation involves avoiding five vices and performing three basic duties.

The five vices are:

lust

covetousness and greed

attachment to the things of this world

anger

pride

The three duties or 'pillars' are:

Nam Japna – 'meditation on God through reciting, chanting, singing and constant remembrance followed by deep study and comprehension of God's Name and virtues'

Kirt Karna – 'to honestly earn one's living by one's physical and mental effort while accepting both pains and pleasures as God's gifts and blessings'

> *Vand Chakna* – 'To share the fruits of one's labour with others before considering oneself'[1]

The ultimate theological authority within Sikhism that provides guidance along the path to *mukti* is the teaching of the eleven gurus. In Sikh belief, there are ten human gurus: Guru Nanak and his nine successors and a written guru, the Sikh holy book, the Adi Granth.[2] As Eleanor Nesbitt explains, 'In Sikh belief all are the physical embodiments of the same Guru. One Sikh analogy for Guru-ship is a flame that lights a succession of torches.'[3]

As the entry on the Adi Granth in the online Sikh encyclopaedia SikhiWiki notes:

> Guru Granth Sahib or Adi Sri Granth Sahib Ji ... (also called the Adi Granth or Adi Guru Darbar) is more than just a scripture of the Sikhs, for the Sikhs treat this Granth (holy book) as their living Guru. The holy text spans 1,430 pages and contains the actual words spoken by the founders of the Sikh religion (the Ten Gurus of Sikhism) and the words of various other Saints from other religions including Hinduism and Islam.

---

1 'Three Pillars', SikhiWiki at https://sikhiwiki.org/index.php/Three_Pill.
2 For an English translation of the Adi Granth, see Ernest Trump, *The Adi Granth: Or Holy Scriptures of the Sikhs* (Munshiram Manoharlal Publishers, 2004).
3 Eleanor Nesbitt, *Sikhism: A Very Short Introduction* (Oxford: OUP, 2005), Kindle edition, Loc.398.

Guru Granth Sahib was given the Guruship by the last of the living Sikh Masters, Guru Gobind Singh Ji in 1708. Guru Gobind Singh said before his demise that the Sikhs were to treat the Granth Sahib as their next Guru. Guru Ji said, '*Sab Sikhan ko hokam hai Guru Manyo Granth*', meaning, 'All Sikhs are commanded to take the Granth as Guru.' So today, if asked, the Sikhs will tell you that they have a total of 11 Gurus (10 in human form and the SGGS [Sri Guru Granth Sahib]).[4]

Alongside the Adi Granth there are two other texts which are also important for Sikh belief and practice. The first of these is the Dasam Granth which contains texts attributed to the tenth guru. These texts are important to many Sikhs, but the Dasam Granth does not have the same authority as the Adi Granth. The second are the Janamsakhis (literally 'birth stories'), writings which provide accounts of the life of Guru Nanak and the foundations of the Sikh religion.

The most well-known symbols of Sikh identity, and what most people think of when they think of Sikhism, are what are known as the 'Five Ks'. These are five physical symbols worn by male Sikhs who have undergone the Sikh initiation ritual or *amrit* as a sign of their dedication to God.

---

4 'Adi Granth,' SikhiWiki at https://www.sikhiwiki.org/index.php/Adi_Granth. The SGGS is an abbreviation for *Sri Guru Granth Sahib*, which is another title for the Adi Granth.

These symbols are:

> *Kesh* (uncut hair)
>
> *Kara* (a steel bracelet)
>
> *Kanga* (a wooden comb)
>
> *Kaccha* – also spelled, *Kachh*, *Kachera* (cotton underwear)
>
> *Kirpan* (steel sword)

As well as keeping their hair uncut, Sikh men (and increasingly women as well) wear a turban as a further sign of their dedication to God. As the article, 'Why do Sikhs wear turbans?' on the *SikhNet* website puts it:

> The turban tells others that we are different. By having a distinct appearance, Sikhs become accountable for their actions. Our distinct Sikh appearance not only makes us think more often about our conduct and its reflection upon a wider society, it also makes us reflect upon our own ideals and how they reflect the teachings of the Sri Guru Granth Sahib. The turban is there to remind us of our connection to God. It frames us as devotees of God and gives us a way to live in gratitude for this gift of recognition. This responsibility of being recognized is also a way of keeping ourselves from self-destructive habits, such as smoking, drinking, etc. The thing is, in our religion our identity goes hand in hand with the turban. There is no other religion in the world that wears a turban as a daily Badge of Identity. The turban of a Sikh is

his or her primary identifying feature. It is
a statement of belonging to the Guru, and
it is a statement of the inner commitment
of the one who wears it.[5]

In summary, for Sikhs, human flourishing means
achieving *mukti*, or liberation from the cycle of death
and rebirth through knowledge of, and union with
God. Flourishing in this way involves avoiding the
five vices and performing the three basic duties. The
distinctive symbols of Sikhism, the wearing of the
'Five Ks' by Sikh men and the turban by Sikh men
(and increasingly Sikh women as well) are signs of
dedication to this way of life and to the God to whom
this way of life leads.

Christianity and the Sikh universe

The Christian faith agrees with Sikhism that there is
one creator God and that to find eternal happiness
human beings need to switch their focus from
themselves to God. It also agrees with the Sikh
rejection of the five vices and the basic way of life set
out in the three pillars of Sikhism (although the focus
of a Christian's meditation and prayer will obviously
be the divine revelation contained in the Old and
New Testaments rather than the teaching of the
Sikh gurus).

However, Christianity also parts company with
Sikhism in a number of respects.

---

5 'Why do Sikhs wear Turbans?', *SikhNet*, http://fateh.
sikhnet.com/s/WhyTurbans.

First, while Christianity and Sikhism both believe in one God, the God described by Sikhism is not the Triune God described in the Bible who, as Jesus Christ, became incarnate for our salvation.

Secondly, from a Christian perspective the Sikh belief that the soul is part of God and that the goal of human existence is for the soul to be merged back into God, 'like the drop of water mingles with the ocean,' as one Sikh writer puts it,[6] gives the soul both too great and too little significance. Too great significance because the soul is part of creation rather than part of the creator; too little significance because the goal of human existence is for the soul, together with the body, to continue to exist in an eternal loving relationship with God rather than simply ceasing to exist.

Thirdly, from a Christian perspective the Sikh doctrine of reincarnation raises the same basic problem as the Hindu and Buddhist doctrines of reincarnation, namely that it fails to do justice to the truth that each person is created by God as a unique being consisting of a material body and an immaterial soul united together, and that this combination of body and soul will endure for eternity.

Fourthly, the previous point means that from a Christian perspective, Sikhism, like Hinduism and Buddhism, misunderstands the fundamental problem facing human beings. For Sikhism, the problem for human beings is that their souls still have a separate existence from God, and the solution is to bring that

_____
6 Sabbar Singh Khalsa, 'Sikh views on Christianity' at www. sikhnet.com/news/sikh-views-christianity.

100

"God wills that we should continue to exist as separate beings in right relationship with him for all eternity."

Christian Jewish Islamic multiverse postmodern materialist Living well deist Hindu Sik

separate existence to an end by diligently following the spiritual path revealed by God through the Sikh gurus.

For Christianity, by contrast, the existence of human beings as creatures separate from God is a good thing. God wills that we should continue to exist as separate beings in right relationship with him for all eternity. The problem is that we are alienated from God because of sin and we are subject to death as a result. The solution is the act of re-creation undertaken by God at the incarnation by which our sinfulness is done away with and because of which our death has been overcome.

Fifthly, this means that Christianity and Sikhism have a different understanding of grace. For Sikhs, grace is the opportunity to possibly obtain *mukti* through diligent adherence to the Sikh spiritual path. For Christians, grace is God having done everything necessary to give us a new life in right relationship with him and making that work of salvation effective in us through the work of the Holy Spirit.

Sikhism and Christianity on human flourishing

In the Sikh universe, human flourishing involves human beings escaping from the cosmic cycle of death and rebirth, through the overcoming of illusion and vice and the merging of the human soul back into the God of which it is a part. The purpose of the Sikh religious tradition is to guide people on this path of escape from salvation and merging with God.

For Christianity, by contrast, there is no need for human beings to escape the cycle of reincarnation since this does not exist. Furthermore, for Christianity human flourishing does not mean the merging of the soul with God, but human beings having a separate joyful existence alongside God forever in the world to come as fruit of the redeeming and sanctifying work of God in Jesus Christ made effective in their lives through the work of the Holy Spirit.

10. Why Christians need to understand the multiverse and why the multiverse exists

It is important for Christians to recognise both the existence and complexity of the religious and philosophical multiverse that now exists in the UK. This is because in order to relate properly to our family members, friends, neighbours, work colleagues and so forth, we have to understand that they are likely to view the world in a variety of different ways. What's more, the majority of them are likely to view the world in a way that is different from the way that orthodox Christianity views it.

There is a tendency among some Christians in the UK today to think that the main challenge to Christianity comes from the critical theory variant of the postmodern worldview. This tendency is understandable given the high public profile and official support for the critical theory approach at the moment, especially in relation to matters to do with race, transgender and same-sex sexual relationships.

However, it obscures the fact that the number of people who actually hold to a postmodern or critical theory approach to the world is very small (although disproportionately represented in academia and the media). A far larger number of people in this country hold, often unconsciously, to a deist or materialist worldview, or hold to a Muslim, Hindu, Buddhist or Sikh worldview, or to one of the other smaller worldviews noted in the introduction.

As has been noted repeatedly in this book, there is great diversity among those who share the same overall worldview. Thus, materialists will disagree with each other over a whole range of matters, as will Muslims and Buddhists. However, this does not mean that overall worldviews do not exist. They do, and Christians need to understand them if they are to understand the world they live in and be effective witnesses for Christ within it.

It is also the case that many people today have an eclectic worldview in which they consciously or unconsciously view the world in a way that is influenced by a number of different worldviews. For example, there are people whose lives are basically shaped by a Christian worldview, but also embrace a pantheist worldview influenced by Hinduism and practice Buddhist meditation techniques as part of their spiritual discipline. As another example, there are those who embrace a materialist or postmodern worldview but whose ethical values, such as a belief in equality, compassion, freedom and progress are in fact derived from Christianity. For a third example, there are LGBTQI+ Muslims who seek to combine a Muslim worldview with a view of sexual freedom and the fluidity of sexual identity derived from postmodernism.

If Christians are to be effective witnesses to people who have such eclectic worldviews, they need to understand the different worldviews that these people are combining and how to address them from a Christian perspective.

"If Christians are to be effective witnesses to people who have such eclectic worldviews, they need to understand the different worldviews that these people are combining and how to address them from a Christian perspective."

Christian
Jewish Islamic
multiverse
postmodern
materialist
Living
well
deist
Hindu
Si

The history of the multiverse

A key question raised by the existence of all these different worldviews is how the multiverse came about. Why is it the case that materialists, Muslims, Buddhists and others exist alongside Christians, both in this country and in the world as a whole?

To answer this question, we have to go back to the beginning of human history.

The biblical account of the beginning of the human story tells us that the original religion of humanity was the worship of the one creator God, as described in Genesis 1 and 2 – the God who subsequently revealed himself to Israel as Yahweh, or in English versions of the Bible 'the Lord'. Thus, in Genesis 4:26, which is intended to give a description of what Gerhard von Rad calls 'the primeval religion of mankind in general,' we are told that in the time of Seth the son of Adam 'men began to call upon the name of the Lord' ('call upon' meaning worship).[1]

The God who created the world had made himself known by means of personal revelation to the first ancestors of the human race (Genesis 1:26–30, 2:15–24, 3:8–19, 4:1–7) and it was this same God, Genesis says, who was worshipped when corporate worship was instituted in the time of Seth (Genesis 4:26).

In the nineteenth century, as part of a general revolt against the historical veracity of the Bible, the biblical picture of religion beginning with the worship of a single creator God came to be widely rejected by

---

1 Gerhard von Rad, *Genesis*, (London: SCM, 1972), 113.

writers on the origins of religion. What came to be held instead was that religion was a purely human construct that had gradually evolved as part of the general development of human culture.

The explanations given by scholars as to the ultimate origins of religion varied from the personification of the forces of nature, the worship of the spiritual forces believed to inhabit human beings and nature as a whole, the propitiation of the spirits of the dead, and the invocation of the spiritual power of the animal symbol (totem) of a particular clan. However, there was general agreement that the religion of early human cultures was primitive and polytheistic, and that monotheism was a late development which emerged as a reaction against this primal polytheism.[2]

This understanding of human religious development has become part of the mental furniture of Western secular culture, something that 'everybody knows'.

However, like many things that 'everybody knows' it can be shown to be wrong. The scholars mentioned above based their work on the assumption that (unlike them) early human beings were ignorant savages, and so their religion must also have been ignorant and savage. Sophisticated ideas such as monotheism must therefore have developed later. The problem with this theory was that it did not do justice to the discoveries about the actual religious beliefs and practices of indigenous peoples around the world as these began to be uncovered by students of ethnography from

---

2 For an introduction to these various theories about the origin of religion, see Wilhelm Schmidt, *The Origin and Growth of Religion* (New York: Humanities Press, 1936).

the nineteenth century onwards. Such peoples had cultures which could be seen to preserve elements of early human culture that predated the developments in later and more sophisticated cultures. When their religion began to be encountered and then studied, it became clear time after time that these cultures had preserved an awareness of a single creator god.

A vivid example of what took place is given by G K Chesterton in his book *The Everlasting Man* (which was published in 1925 and uses the language of his day):

> A missionary was preaching to a very wild tribe of polytheists, who had told him all their polytheistic tales, and telling them in return of the existence of the one good God who is spirit and judges men by spiritual standards. And there was a sudden buzz of excitement among these stolid barbarians, as at somebody who was letting out a secret, and they cried to each other, 'Atahocan! He is speaking of Atahocan!'[3]

As Chesterton goes on to say:

> ...there are any number of similar examples. They all testify to the unmistakable psychology of a thing taken for granted, as distinct from a thing talked about. There is a striking example in a tale taken down word for word from a

---

3 G. K. Chesterton, *The Everlasting Man* (San Francisco: Ignatius Press, 1993), 88.

Red Indian in California, which starts out with hearty legendary and literary relish: 'The sun is the father and ruler of the heavens. He is the big chief. The moon is his wife and the stars are their children;' and so on through a most ingenious and complicated story, in the middle of which is a sudden parenthesis saying that the sun and moon have to do something because 'It is ordered that way by the Great Spirit Who lives above the place of all.' That is exactly the attitude of most paganism towards God. He is something assumed and forgotten and remembered by accident; a habit possibly not peculiar to pagans.[4]

In addition to the evidence provided by the cultures of indigenous peoples, scholars also found evidence for original belief in monotheism by studying the later development of language and culture around the world. For example, as Robert Brow notes, study of the Indo-European language group shows an awareness of the one creator God among all the Indo-European peoples:

His first name was Dyaus Pitar ('divine father') which is the same as the Greek Zeus Pater, the Latin Jupiter or Deus, the early German Tiu or Ziu and Norse Tyr. Another name was 'the heavenly one' (Sanskrit *varuna*, Greek *ouranos*), or 'the friend' (Sanskrit *mitra*, Persian *mithra*). By metaphor and simile other names

_____
4 Chesterton, *Everlasting Man*, 88.

were added. God is called 'the sun,' 'the powerful one' and 'the guardian of order.'[5]

The peoples involved eventually became polytheistic, but the linguistic evidence for an original monotheism remains.

In similar fashion, the evidence from China indicates that the earliest form of Chinese religion that we know about involved the worship of the one supreme sky-god known as Shang-Ti or Hao-Tien who was, as Corduan writes, 'sovereign, eternal, immutable, all-powerful, all-knowing, ever-present, infinite, love, holy, full of grace, good, faithful, merciful, compassionate, just, righteous and wise.'[6] When Confucius and other Chinese writers refer to heaven (as in the phrase 'the mandate of heaven'), the evidence suggests that they are referring periphrastically to this god. As Chinese religion developed, the worship of Shang-Ti faded into the background, but sacrifice was offered to him three times a year by the Chinese Emperor right until the end of Imperial China in 1911.

These kind of examples of evidence for primeval monotheism from all round the world were compiled by the Scottish scholar Andrew Lang in his book

---

5 Robert Brow, 'The Original Religion of Man' in *Religion: Origins and Ideas* available at http://brow.on.ca/Books/Religion/Religion1.html.
6 Winfried Corduan, *In the beginning God: A fresh look at the case for original monotheism* (Nashville: B&H Academic, 2013), 333, citing Chan Kei Thong and Charlene Fu, *Finding God in Ancient China* (Grand Rapids: Zondervan, 2009), 88–106.

The Making of Religion, first published in 1898.[7] They were then set out in exhaustive detail by the Austrian Catholic scholar Wilhelm Schmidt in the 11,000 pages of his twelve-volume *Der Ursprung der Gottesidee* (*The Origin of the Idea of God*) which was published from 1912 onwards.[8] Further study since their time has confirmed rather than overthrown their findings. The evidence of historical, ethnographic and linguistic study confirms the biblical idea that the original religion of mankind was the worship of one creator god.

The existence of this evidence raises the issue of the ultimate origin of this religion. We know it existed, but why did it exist? As we have seen, the biblical answer is that God revealed himself personally to the earliest human beings, and this biblical answer is supported by the ethnographical evidence which time after time says that the first ancestor(s) of the people in question learned about God from God, and then passed this information on to their subsequent descendants.

To quote Schmidt:

> The bottom line is that the reports we have from the adherents of the oldest religions themselves are not only merely disinclined towards the supposition that the religions were created by seeking and searching human beings; rather,

---

7 Andrew Lang, *The Making of Religion* (London: Longmans, Green and Co., 1909).
8 Wilhelm Schmidt, *Der Ursprung der Gottesidee*, Vols I–XII (Munster: Aschendorff, 1912–1955).

worse yet, they do not even mention it with a single word. All their affirmative responses are directed to the side of divine revelation: it is God Himself Who taught humans what to believe about Him, how to venerate Him, and how they should obey the expression of His will.[9]

As Schmidt further argues, the sort of experience to which these testimonies bear witness is required to explain the evidence that we have concerning primeval religion:

Something of such intense force must have come upon these most ancient human beings in an encounter that became an all-encompassing destabilising experience, penetrating their entire being to its innermost core, so that immediately, due to its overpowering might, it gave rise to the unity and comprehensiveness that we observe, in these, the oldest of religions.

This 'something' could not have been merely a subjective process inside of the human being himself; for then it could not have held either the power or the complete blueprint of these, the oldest of religions. There would have been no way in which the clarity and solidity of their outlook of faith, as well as the cultural forms associated with it, could have been implemented. Neither could it have been

9 Schmidt, *Der Ursprung der Gottesidee*, Vol. VI (1935), 480.

a purely material thing or event, no matter how unusual it may have appeared. For then it would have become increasingly inexplicable how mere material stuff could act on the combined personhood of these ancient people with the power, firmness, and clarity that we admire in these, the oldest of religions.

No, it must have been a powerful mighty person, who stepped toward them, and who was able to chain their intellects with illuminating truths, to bind their wills with high and noble precepts, and to win their hearts with enticing beauty and goodness. And again, this person could not have been an inner chimera or phantasm of mere human origin because such an entity could not even have come close to possessing sufficient actual power to cause the effects we see in these, the oldest of religions. Instead, it must have been a person who came to them as a genuine reality from outside of them, and it is precisely the power of this reality that convinced them and conquered them.[10]

If the evidence shows that the earliest religion of humankind was monotheism based on direct divine revelation, then why is there the diversity of religions and philosophies that we see today. What happened?

---

10 Schmidt, *Der Ursprung der Gottesidee*, Vol.VI (1935), 492.

The answer seems to be that the present state of affairs emerged in several stages.

First, there was the emergence of polytheism, a development which saw the one god of monotheism become part of a pantheon of different divine beings. Thus, Zeus, the divine father, is still worshipped, but becomes only one among a range of Greek deities and the same is true of Tyr who ends up as a fairly minor Norse deity. Alongside this development there was also the development of idolatry as both people (such as the Egyptian Pharaohs), and created objects such as statues, came to be seen as the places where the gods manifested themselves on earth, and therefore became the objects of worship in their own right.

Secondly, in the sixth century BC, there was what has been described by Karl Jaspers as the 'axial age' – a time which saw the emergence not only, as we have seen, of Vedanta Hinduism and Buddhism, but also of Jainism in India, Zoroastrianism in Persia, and Confucianism and Taoism in China.[11]

These religions all seem to have emerged as a result of a revolt against the religious teaching, and also the economic and political power, of the priesthoods of the existing polytheistic religions in India, China and Persia. They introduced a range of religious ideas and practices, but none of them marked a return to a simple creational monotheism. Instead, these new forms of religion were marked by pantheism, or atheism, or agnosticism, or, in the case of Zoroastrianism, a dualism between the good creator god Ahura

_____
11 See Karl Jaspers, *The Origin and Goal of History* (London: Routledge, 2012).

Mazda and the co-equal and co-eternal evil deity Ahura Mainyu.

The sixth-century revolt against polytheistic religion just described seems also to have sparked off the revolt against polytheistic forms of religion which can be found in Greek and later Roman philosophy. This movement, while challenging existing forms of religion, once again failed to produce a return to creational monotheism.

Thirdly, in the seventh century, Islam emerged as a reaction against Arabian polytheism. As we have noted, Islam is an uncompromisingly monotheistic form of religion, and it may have had its roots in ancient Arabian monotheism. It is theologically problematic because although it claims to be in line with the monotheistic religion taught in the Old and New Testaments, this is not in fact the case.

Fourthly, Sikhism emerged out of the Hindu tradition in the fifteenth century. It too is monotheistic, but, as noted in chapter 9, its form of monotheism also raises a range of theological problems due to its attempt to combine monotheism, with monism and reincarnation.

Fifthly, deism, followed by materialism and postmodernism, developed as a revolt against Christian monotheism from the end of seventeenth century onwards.

This leaves us with Judaism and Christianity. To understand their emergence, we need to note that both the Christian faith, and a range of primeval religious traditions from around the world, bear witness to the fact that the creative activity of the single good creator God has been undermined by the work of an evil spiritual power, with the result that the world as it now exists is not how it was originally meant to be. For example, as Corduan notes, the creation account of the Lenape people in the Eastern United States declares that after the Great Manitou created the heavens and the earth:

> Everyone was content. Unfortunately, the harmony of the world was eventually disrupted by the appearance of an evil magician who brought strife, natural disasters, sickness and death to all people.[12]

What the Bible tells us is that in order to rectify the disharmony introduced into his good creation by this evil power (what Christian theology calls the devil), God revealed himself to Abraham and established a covenant relationship with him and his descendants (the people of Israel) through which all the families of the earth would be blessed (Genesis 12:1–3).

The God worshipped by Abraham is identified in Genesis 17:1 as El Shaddai, God Almighty. He is further identified in Genesis 14:22 as 'the Lord God Most High, maker of heaven and earth' – the same deity of whom Melchizedek was a priest (Genesis 14:18–19) and, in the context of Genesis, the same almighty creator God described in the creation stories in Genesis 1 and 2. What we learn from this is that a continuing form of pure monotheistic religion had survived among people like Melchizedek, and that

---

12 Corduan, In the beginning God, 207.

Abraham, who had been a polytheist (Joshua 24:2) converted to this pure monotheism after his personal encounter with God.

The Old Testament then goes on to tell us that this same creator God subsequently appeared to Moses at the burning bush (Exodus 3:13–15, 6:2–4), rescued the people of Israel from Egypt, and established them in the land that he had promised to Abraham that he would give them. The rest of the Old Testament is the story of how this God maintained his relationship with the people of Israel in spite of their constant rebellion against him. It tells how he spoke to them through a series of prophets – they warned the people to worship God alone and to live in obedience to God's laws, and they promised that God would act in new way to fulfil the covenant of universal blessing made with Abraham.

The New Testament tells the story of how this promise was fulfilled. The creator God took human nature upon himself in the person of Jesus Christ (John 1:1–18, Hebrews 1:1–14). This began a process of cosmic renewal through Christ's death and resurrection and the pouring out of the Holy Spirit on the day of Pentecost (Romans 8:1–25), a process which will culminate in the coming of a 'new heaven and a new earth' (Revelation 21:1). Here God's people, drawn from all the nations of the earth will dwell with him forever, and 'death shall be no more, neither shall there be mourning, nor crying, nor pain anymore, for the former things have passed away' (Revelation 21:4).

As we have seen in chapters 1 and 2, the difference between Judaism and Christianity is that Judaism accepts the witness of the Hebrew Bible/Old Testament, but not the witness of the New Testament, while Christianity accepts both. It is for this reason that it is in Christianity alone that the true and full knowledge of who God is, and what he has done in the past and will do in the future, has been passed down through the centuries and continues to exist today.

What this means is that the story of the development of the multiverse is a story of degeneration and regeneration. It is a story of degeneration that tells how the knowledge of the one creator God has gradually become lost during the course of human history. It is a story of regeneration that tells how God has acted to restore and deepen this knowledge through the history of Israel, the incarnation of Jesus Christ and the work of the Spirit, as part of his overall regeneration of the created order in the face of its corruption by the activity of the devil and the human alienation from God that has resulted from it.

The development of Islam and Sikhism represent genuine attempts to restore monotheism, but the particular forms of monotheism that resulted are flawed for the reasons previously noted, and they do not give an accurate account of the nature of God and his activity in the world.

11. Living well in the multiverse

Once we have understood what the multiverse of worldviews looks like, and how it has emerged, the final challenge we face is how we should live well within it. In my view, living well in this multiverse involves three key activities: developing understanding, standing firm and reaching out.

If we are to live well in the multiverse, by standing firm for Christ and reaching out to those who do not yet believe in him, we first of all need to develop an understanding of why it is that the multiverse exists (as discussed in the previous chapter) and the particular form of the conceptual multiverse that our family, friends and neighbours inhabit (as discussed in the preceding chapters). As we also noted, to reach out to them effectively, we have to start from where they are, and to do this we have to understand the universe that they think they live in.

Standing firm involves holding on to the truth about God and the human situation before God that God has revealed and that the orthodox Christian tradition has preserved. The history of the growth of the multiverse shows that it is all too easy for the truth about God to become forgotten and distorted, and the Christian calling is to stand find in 'the faith which was once for all delivered to the saints' (Jude 3) so that, as far as possible, this does not continue to happen.

Standing firm also involves living in the way that God wants his human creatures to live. As the all-good and all-wise creator of the universe, God has laid down how we should live and the Christian vocation is to be faithful in living this way, obeying all that God has commanded us to do, and rejecting all that God has commanded us not to do.

In the words of Os Guinness:

> The church of Jesus can never be the church without both faith and faithfulness, and both of them in a form that is strong to the point of being stubborn. The supreme challenge of the hour for the church of Jesus in the advanced modern world is to so live and speak as witnesses to our Lord that, as in the motto of the US Marines, we are *'Semper Fi'* – always Found Faithful. Rarely in two thousand years of Christian history has that calling been so tested as it is in our time. Come threats of death or seductive temptations to an easy life, our task is to stand faithful to our Lord in every moment of our lives and faithful to our last breath.[1]

Reaching out involves relating to others who do not yet know or accept the Christian worldview in obedience to Jesus' commission to his disciples in Matthew 28:19–20: 'Go therefore and make disciples of all nations, baptising them in the name of the Father and of the Son and of the Holy Spirit, teaching them to observe all that I have commanded you.'

---

1 Os Guinness, *Impossible People* (Downers Grove: IVP, 2016), Kindle edition, Loc. 357.

"As the all-good and all-wise creator of the universe, God has laid down how we should live and the Christian vocation is to be faithful in living this way, obeying all that God has commanded us to do, and rejecting all that God has commanded us not to do."

Christian Jewish Islamic multiverse postmodern materialist Living well deal Hind

What such obedience should mean in practice has been helpfully summarised by the great twentieth-century theology missiologist Lesslie Newbigin who makes four key points in his book, *The Gospel in a Pluralist Society*.

First, there needs to be *recognition*. We must discern and acknowledge the signs of the work of God in the lives of those who are not yet Christians, who are God's creatures and the recipients of his grace, even if this is not yet the saving grace that leads to salvation:

> We shall expect, look for, and welcome all the signs of the grace of God at work in the lives of those who do not know Jesus as Lord. In this, of course, we shall be following the example of Jesus, who was so eager to welcome the evidences of faith in those outside the household of Israel. This kind of expectancy and welcome is an implication of the greatness of God's grace as it has been shown to us in Jesus. For Jesus is the personal presence of that creative word by which all that exists was made and is sustained in being. He comes to the world as no stranger but as the source of the world's life. He is the true light of the world, and that light shines into every corner of the world in spite of all that seeks to shut it out. In our contact with people who do not acknowledge Jesus as Lord, our first business, our first privilege, is to seek out and to welcome all the reflections of that one true light in

the lives of those we meet.[2]

Secondly, there must be *co-operation*. Christians need to be:

> ...eager to cooperate with people of all faiths and ideologies in all projects which are in line with the Christian's understanding of God's purpose in history. I have repeatedly made the point that the heart of the faith of a Christian is the belief that the true meaning of the story of which our lives are a part is that which is made known in the biblical narrative. The human story is one which we share with all other human beings – past, present, and to come. We cannot opt out of the story. We cannot take control of the story. It is under the control of the infinitely patient God and Father of our Lord Jesus Christ. Every day of our lives we have to make decisions about the part we will play in the story, decisions which we cannot take without regard to the others who share the story. They may be Christians, Muslims, Hindus, secular humanists, Marxists, or of some other persuasion. They will have different understandings of the meaning and end of the story, but along the way there will be many issues in which we can agree about what should be done. There are struggles for justice and for freedom

---

2 Lesslie Newbigin, *The Gospel in a Pluralist Society* (London: SPCK, 1989), 180.

in which we can and should join hands with those of other faiths and ideologies to achieve specific goals, even though we know that the ultimate goal is Christ and his coming in glory and not what our collaborators imagine.[3]

Thirdly, co-operation will open the door for *dialogue*:

It is precisely in this kind of shared commitment to the business of the world that the context for true dialogue is provided. As we work together with people of other commitments, we shall discover the places where our ways must separate. Here is where real dialogue may begin. It is a real dialogue about real issues. It is not just a sharing of religious experience, though it may include this. At heart it will be a dialogue about the meaning and goal of the human story. If we are doing what we ought to be doing as Christians, the dialogue will be initiated by our partners, not by ourselves. They will be aware of the fact that while we share with them in commitment to some immediate project, our action is set in a different context from theirs. It has a different motivation. It looks to a different goal.[4]

Fourthly, Christians need to be willing *to tell the Christian story*, content to leave the outcome to God:

3 Newbigin, *Gospel in a Pluralist Society*, 181.
4 Newbigin, *Gospel in a Pluralist Society*, 181.

The essential contribution of the Christian to the dialogue will simply be the telling of the story, the story of Jesus, the story of the Bible. The story is itself, as Paul says, the power of God for salvation. The Christian must tell it, not because she lacks respect for the many excellences of her companions – many of whom may be better, more godly, more worthy of respect than she is. She tells it simply as one who's been chosen and called by God to be part of the company which is entrusted with the story. It is not her business to convert the others. She will indeed – out of love for them – long that they may come to share the joy that she knows and pray that they may indeed do so. But it is only the Holy Spirit of God who can so touch the hearts and consciences of the others that they are brought to accept the story as true and to put their trust in Jesus. This will always be a mysterious work of the Spirit, often in ways which no third party will ever understand. The Christian will pray that it may be so, and she will seek faithfully both to tell the story and – as part of a Christian congregation – so conduct her life as to embody the truth of the story. But she will not imagine that it is her responsibility to ensure that the other is persuaded. That is in God's hands.[5]

---

5 Newbigin, *Gospel in a Pluralist Society*, 181.

It is as Christians understand the multiverse in which they live, remain faithful to God in their belief and practice, and reach out to others in the way that Newbigin describes that they will best be able to fulfil their calling to be 'God's fellow workers' (1 Corinthians 3:9) furthering God's good purposes for the world that he has made.

Appendix 1: Why the incarnation needed to happen and why we can be confident that it did

As we have seen in the course of this book, at the heart of the Christian worldview is the belief that the second person of the Trinity, God the Son, the eternal image of God the Father, took human nature upon himself in the person of Jesus Christ in order to save the human race.

This belief raises two questions – why the incarnation needed to happen and whether we can be confident that it did.

In this appendix I want to give answers to these two questions using extracts from the works of the early Christian bishop and theologian Athanasius and C S Lewis.

Athanasius, *Of the Incarnation of the Word*

Athanasius wrote his book *Of the Incarnation of the Word* in the early years of the fourth century. As he explains at the beginning of this work, his purpose in writing it is to ensure that his readers:

> ...may neither fail to know the cause of the bodily appearing of the Word of the Father, so high and so great, nor think it a consequence of His own nature that the Saviour has worn a body; but that being incorporeal by nature, and Word from the beginning, He has yet of the loving-

kindness and goodness of His own Father been manifested to us in a human body for our salvation.[1]

By the term 'Word' he means God the Son, whom he describes as the 'Word' in line with teaching of the opening verses of John's Gospel (John 1:1–18).

In a famous passage in chapters 13–14, Athanasius goes on to describe the reason the incarnation needed to happen as follows:

> So then, men having thus become brutalised, and demoniacal deceit thus clouding every place, and hiding the knowledge of the true God, what was God to do? To keep still silence at so great a thing, and suffer men to be led astray by demons and not to know God? And what was the use of man having been originally made in God's image? For it had been better for him to have been made simply like a brute animal, than, once made rational, for him to live the life of the brutes. Or where was any necessity at all for his receiving the idea of God to begin with? For if he be not fit to receive it even now, it were better it had not been given him at first. Or what profit to God Who has made them, or what glory to Him could it be, if men, made by Him, do

1 Athanasius, 'On the Incarnation', Ch.1 in Archibald Robertson, ed., *The Nicene and Post-Nicene Fathers*, 2nd series, vol. IV (Edinburgh and Grand Rapids: T&T Clark, Eerdmans, 1998), 36.

not worship Him, but think that others are their makers? For God thus proves to have made these for others instead of for Himself. Once again, a merely human king does not let the lands he has colonised pass to others to serve them, nor go over to other men; but he warns them by letters, and often sends to them by friends, or, if need be, he comes in person, to put them to rebuke in the last resort by his presence, only that they may not serve others and his own work be spent for nought. Shall not God much more spare His own creatures, that they be not led astray from Him and serve things of nought? Especially since such going astray proves the cause of their ruin and undoing, and since it was unfitting that they should perish which had once been partakers of God's image. What then was God to do? Or what was to be done save the renewing of that which was in God's image, so that by it men might once more be able to know Him? But how could this have come to pass save by the presence of the very image of God, our Lord Jesus Christ? For by men's means it was impossible, since they are but made after an image; nor by angels either, for not even they are (God's) images. Whence the Word of God came in His own person, that, as He was the Image of the Father, He might be able to create afresh the man after the image. But, again, it could not else have taken place had not death and corruption been done away. Whence He took, in natural fitness, a mortal body, that while death might in it be once for all done away, men made after His Image might once more be renewed. None other then was sufficient for this need, save the Image of the Father.

For as, when the likeness painted on a panel has been effaced by stains from without, he whose likeness it is must needs come once more to enable the portrait to be renewed on the same wood: for, for the sake of his picture, even the mere wood on which it is painted is not thrown away, but the outline is renewed upon it; in the same way also the most holy Son of the Father, being the Image of the Father, came to our region to renew man once made in His likeness, and find him, as one lost, by the remission of sins; as He says Himself in the Gospels: 'I came to find and to save the lost.' [Luke 19:10] Whence He said to the Jews also: 'Except a man be born again,' [John 3:3], not meaning, as they thought, birth from woman, but speaking of the soul born and created anew in the likeness of God's image. But since wild idolatry and godlessness occupied the world, and the knowledge of God was hid, whose part was it to teach the world concerning the Father? Man's, might one say? But it was not in man's power to penetrate everywhere beneath the sun; for neither had they the physical strength to run so far, nor would they be able to claim credence in this matter, nor were they sufficient by themselves to withstand the deceit and impositions of evil spirits. For where all were smitten and confused in soul from demoniacal deceit, and the vanity of idols, how was it possible for them to win over man's soul and man's mind – whereas they cannot even see them? Or how can a man convert what he does not see? But perhaps one might say creation was enough; but if creation were enough, these great evils would never have come to pass. For creation was there already, and all the same, men were grovelling in the same error concerning God. Who, then, was needed, save the Word of God, that sees both soul and mind, and that gives movement to all things in creation, and by them makes known the Father? For He who by His own Providence and ordering of all things was teaching men concerning the Father, He it was that could renew this same teaching as well. How, then, could this have been done? Perhaps one might say that the same means were open as before, for Him to show forth the truth about the Father once more by means of the work of creation. But this was no longer a sure means. Quite the contrary; for men missed seeing this before, and have turned their eyes no longer upward but downward. Whence, naturally, willing to profit men, He sojourns here as man, taking to Himself a body like the others, and from things of earth, that is by the works of His body [He teaches them], so that they who would not know Him from His Providence and rule over all things, may even from the works done by His actual body know the Word of God which is in the body, and through Him the Father.[2]

The key thing to note about what Athanasius says in these chapters is that although they were written some 1,700 years ago, the explanation of the reason for the incarnation he offers is still persuasive in the light of the knowledge that we have today and that we have briefly surveyed in this book.

C S Lewis, *Mere Christianity*

Turning to the second question of whether we can be confident that the incarnation actually happened, a compelling answer is given by C S Lewis in *Mere Christianity*. In a celebrated passage in chapter 3, he puts forward what has become known as the 'Lewis trilemma' which says that Jesus was either bad, mad, or God. The evidence we have concerning Jesus' words and actions tell us that Jesus was either Lord (in other words, God), or a bad man, or a lunatic. Since the evidence indicates that he was neither a bad man, nor a lunatic, he must be Lord. In Lewis' own words:

---

2 Athanasius, 'On the Incarnation', Chs.13–14 in Robertson, *Nicene and Post-Nicene Fathers*, 44-44.

...what did God do? First of all, He left us conscience, the sense of right and wrong: and all through history there have been people trying (some of them very hard) to obey it. None of them ever quite succeeded. Secondly, He sent the human race what I call good dreams: I mean those queer stories scattered all through the heathen religions about a god who dies and comes to life again and, by his death, has somehow given new life to men. Thirdly, He selected one particular people and spent several centuries hammering into their heads the sort of God He was – that there was only one of Him and that He cared about right conduct. Those people were the Jews, and the Old Testament gives an account of the hammering process.

Then comes the real shock. Among these Jews there suddenly turns up a man who goes about talking as if He was God. He claims to forgive sins. He says He has always existed. He says He is coming to judge the world at the end of time. Now let us get this clear. Among Pantheists, like the Indians, anyone might say that he was a part of God, or one with God: there would be nothing very odd about it. But this man, since He was a Jew, could not mean that kind of God. God, in their language, meant the Being outside the world who had made it and was infinitely different from anything else. And when you have grasped that, you will see that what this man said was, quite simply, the most shocking thing that has ever been uttered by human lips.

One part of the claim tends to slip past us unnoticed because we have heard it so often that we no longer see what it amounts to. I mean the claim to forgive sins: any sins. Now unless the speaker is God, this is really so preposterous as to be comic. We can all understand how a man forgives offences against himself. You tread on my toe and I forgive you, you steal my money and I forgive you. But what should we make of a man, himself unrobbed and untrodden on, who announced that he forgave you for treading on other men's toes and stealing other men's money? Asinine fatuity is the kindest description we should give of his conduct. Yet this is what Jesus did. He told people that their sins were forgiven, and never waited to consult all the other people whom their sins had undoubtedly injured. He unhesitatingly behaved as if He was the party chiefly concerned, the person chiefly offended in all offences. This makes sense only if He really was the God whose laws are broken and whose love is wounded in every sin. In the mouth of any speaker who is not God, these words would imply what I can only regard as a silliness and conceit unrivalled by any other character in history.

Yet (and this is the strange, significant thing) even His enemies, when they read the Gospels, do not usually get the impression of silliness and conceit. Still less do unprejudiced readers. Christ says that He is 'humble and meek', and we believe Him; not noticing that, if He were merely a man, humility and meekness are the very last characteristics we could attribute to some of His sayings.

I am trying here to prevent anyone saying the really foolish thing that people often say about Him: 'I'm ready to accept Jesus as a great moral teacher, but I don't accept His claim to be God.' That is the one thing we must not say. A man who was merely a man and said the sort of things Jesus said would not be a great moral teacher. He would either be a lunatic – on a level with the man who says he is a poached egg – or else he would be the Devil of Hell. You must make your choice. Either this man was, and is, the Son of God: or else a madman or something worse. You can shut Him up for a fool, you can spit at Him and kill Him as a demon; or you can fall at His feet and call Him Lord and God. But let us not come with any patronising nonsense about His being a great human teacher. He has not left that open to us. He did not intend to.[3]

3 Lewis, *Mere Christianity*, 51–52. For a cogent defence of Lewis' argument against criticisms of it, see David A. Horner '*Aut Deus aut Malus Homo*' in David Baggett, Gary Habermas and Jerry Walls eds., *C. S. Lewis as Philosopher* (Downers Grove: IVP Academic, 2008), Ch.4.

Appendix 2: G K Chesterton on the reconciliation of the two halves of the human mind

In his book *The Everlasting Man* from which I quoted in chapter 10, the Catholic journalist and apologist G K Chesterton tells the story of the development of humanity and human civilisation from a Christian perspective.

In the course of his book, he explains that there have been two conflicting tendencies throughout human history, the human delight in telling stories and the human search for truth. At the end of the book, he then notes that only the Christian worldview harmonises and satisfies these two tendencies by containing the ultimate story (the truth myth) which finally reveals the truth about the nature of things and fulfils the narrative instinct that a story needs to contain a beginning and an end, and that what happens at the end needs to be determined by the choices that are freely made in between.

To quote Chesterton, the Christian worldview:

> ...is the reconciliation because it is the realisation both of mythology and philosophy. It is a story and in that sense one of a hundred stories; only it is a true story. It is a philosophy and in that sense one of a hundred philosophies; only it is a philosophy that is like life. But above all, it is a reconciliation because it is something that can only be called the philosophy of stories. That normal narrative instinct

which produced all the fairy tales is something that is neglected by all the philosophies – except one. The Faith is the justification of that popular instinct; the finding of a philosophy for it or the analysis of the philosophy in it. Exactly as a man in an adventure story has to pass various tests to save his life, so the man in this philosophy has to pass several tests and save his soul. In both there is an idea of free will operating under conditions of design; in other words, there is an aim, and it is the business of a man to aim at it; we therefore watch to see whether he will hit it. Now this deep and democratic and dramatic instinct is derided and dismissed in all the other philosophies. For all the other philosophies avowedly end where they begin; and it is the definition of a story that it ends differently; that it begins in one place and ends in another. From Buddha and his wheel to Akhen Aten and his disc,[1] from Pythagoras with his abstraction of number[2] to Confucius with his religion of routine,[3] there is not one of them that does not in some way sin

---

[1] Akhen Aten was an Egyptian Pharaoh who tried to impose on Egypt the worship of the one god Aten symbolised by an image of the disc of the sun.

[2] Pythagoras was a classical Greek philosopher whose philosophy is said to have emphasised the philosophical significance of numbers and which also involved a belief in reincarnation akin to that in Eastern religion.

[3] Confucius was a Chinese philosopher whose collected sayings or *Analects* became the foundation for classical Chinese philosophy and civilisation.

against the soul of a story. There is none of them that really grasps this human notion of the tale, the test, the adventure; the ordeal of the free man. Each of them starves the story-telling instinct, so to speak, and does something to spoil human life considered as a romance; either by fatalism (pessimist or optimist) and that destiny that is the death of adventure; or by indifference and that detachment that is the death of drama; or by a fundamental scepticism that dissolves the actors into atoms; or by a materialistic limitation blocking the vista of moral consequences; or a mechanical recurrence making even moral tests monotonous; or a bottomless relativity making even practical tests insecure.[4]

'To sum up,' he says:

...the sanity of the world was restored and the soul of man offered salvation by something which did indeed satisfy the two warring tendencies of the past; which had never been satisfied in full and most certainly never satisfied together. It met the mythological search for romance by being a story and the philosophical search for truth by being a true story. That is why the ideal figure had to be a historical character, as nobody had ever felt Adonis or Pan to be a historical character. But that is also why the historical character

_____
4 Chesterton, *Everlasting Man*, 246.

had to be the ideal figure; and even fulfil many of the functions given to these other ideal figures; why he was at once the sacrifice and the feast, why he could be shown under the emblems of the growing vine or the rising sun. The more deeply we think of the matter the more we shall conclude that, if there be indeed a God, his creation could hardly have reached any other culmination than this granting of a real romance to the world. Otherwise, the two sides of the human mind could never have touched at all; and the brain of man would have remained cloven and double; one lobe of it dreaming impossible dreams and the other repeating invariable calculations. The picture-makers would have remained for ever painting the portrait of nobody. The sages would have remained for ever adding up numerals that came to nothing. It was that abyss that nothing but an incarnation could cover; a divine embodiment of our dreams; and he stands above that chasm whose name is more than priest and older even than Christendom; Pontifex Maximus, the mightiest maker of a bridge.[5]

5 Chesterton, *Everlasting Man*, 248.

Bibliography

American Humanist Association, Humanist Manifesto II at: https://americanhumanist.org/what-is-humanism/manifesto2/

Athanasius, On the Incarnation, Ch.1 in Archibald Robertson (ed), *The Nicene and Post-Nicene Fathers*, 2nd series, vol. IV (Edinburgh and Grand Rapids: T&T Clark, Eerdmans, 1998)

David Baggett, Gary Habermas and Jerry Walls (eds), *C. S. Lewis as Philosopher* (Downers Grove: IVP Academic, 2008)

Andy Bannister, *Do Christians and Muslims Worship the Same God?* (London: Inter-Varsity Press, 2021)

David Birnbaum, *Jews, Church & Civilization* Volume III (Millennium Education Foundation, 2005)

Emile Bréhier, *The History of Philosophy* (Chicago: Chicago University Press, 1967)

Robert Brow, Religion: Origins and Ideas, at http://brow.on.ca/Books/Religion/Religion1.html

G. K. Chesterton, *The Everlasting Man* (San Francisco: Ignatius Press, 1993)

Winfried Corduan, *In the Beginning God: A fresh look at the case for original monotheism* (Nashville, B&H Academic, 2013)

Winfried Corduan et al, Eastern Religions, *Areopagus Journal* 9:3 (2009)

N. J. Darwood, *The Koran* (London: Penguin Classics, 2014)

Richard Dawkins, *The Blind Watchmaker* (New York: W. W. Norton, 1986)

Os Guinness, *Impossible People* (Downers Grove: IVP, 2016)

John Haldane, *Possible Worlds and Other Essays* (London: Chatto and Windus, 1927)

Stephen Hawking, *The Grand Design* (London: Bantam, 2010)

Karl Jaspers, *The Origin and Goal of History* (London: Routledge, 2012)

Jewish Virtual Library, https://www.jewishvirtuallibrary.org

J. N. D. Kelly, *Early Christian Creeds* 5th ed (London and New York: Continuum, 2000)

Peter Kreeft, *Fundamentals of the Faith* (San Francisco: Ignatius Press, 1988)

Andrew Lang, *The Making of Religion* (London: Longmans, Green & Co., 1898)

C. S. Lewis, *Mere Christianity* (Glasgow: Fount, 1984)

C. S. Lewis, *The Magician's Nephew* (London: Harper Collins, 2009)

Donald Lopez, *Buddhist Scriptures* (London: Penguin,

2004)

Martin Luther, *Three Treatises* (Philadelphia: Fortress Press, 1978)

Martin Luther, Small Catechism, in Mark Noll (ed), *Confessions and Catechisms of the Reformation* (Vancouver: Regent College Publishing, 2004)

Jean-François Lyotard, *The Postmodern Condition* (Minneapolis: University of Minnesota Press, 1984)

Alberto Manguel, *Maimonides: Faith in Reason* (Jewish Lives) (New Haven: Yale University Press, 2023)

Laura Mersini-Houghton, *Before the Big Bang: The Origin of Our Universe from the Multiverse* (London: Bodley Head, 2022)

Stephen Meyer, *The Return of the God Hypothesis* (London: Harper One, 2021)

Lesslie Newbigin, *The Gospel in a Pluralist Society* (London: SPCK, 1989)

Eleanor Nisbett, *Sikhism: A Very Short Introduction* (Oxford: OUP, 2005)

J. I. Packer, *Knowing God* (London: Hodder and Stoughton, 1973)

William Paley, *Natural Theology* (Oxford: OUP, 2008)

Helen Pluckrose and James Lindsay, *Cynical Theories* (London: Swift Press, 2020)

John Polkinghorne, *One World* (London: SPCK, 1986)

Alexander Pope, *An Essay on Man* (Indianapolis and New York: Bobs-Merrill, 1965)

Gerhard von Rad, *Genesis*, (London: SCM, 1972

Bertrand Russell, *Mysticism and Logic* (New York: Barnes and Noble, 2017)

Wilhelm Schmidt, *Der Ursprung der Gottesidee* (Munster: Aschendorff, 1912–1955)

Wilhelm Schmidt, *The Origin and Growth of Religion* (New York: Humanities Press, 1936)

SikhiWiki at https://www.sikhiwiki.org/

SikhNet at https://www.sikhnet.com/

James Sire, *The Universe Next Door* 6th ed (Downers Grove: IVP, 2020)

Christian Smith and Melinda Denton, *Soul Searching: The Religious and Spiritual Lives of American Teenagers* (Oxford: OUP, 2005)

Charles Taylor, *A Secular Age* (Cambridge MA: Belknap Press, 2007)

Charles Taylor, *The Ethics of Authenticity* (Cambridge MA: Harvard University Press, 1992)

Ernest Trump, *The Adi Granth: Or Holy Scriptures of the Sikhs* (Munshiram Manoharlal Publishers, 2004)

Kevin Vanhoozer (ed), *The Cambridge Companion to Postmodern Theology* (Cambridge: CUP, 2003)

R. C. Zaehner, *Hindu Scriptures* (London and New York: Everyman, 1992)

Permissions

Latimer Trust is grateful for the following permissions:

Scripture quotations from the Revised Standard Version of the Bible, copyright © 1946, 1952, and 1971 the Division of Christian Education of the National Council of the Churches of Christ in the United States of America. Used by permission. All rights reserved.

Mere Christianity by C.S. Lewis copyright © 1942, 1943, 1944, 1952 C.S. Lewis Pte. Ltd. Extract reprinted by permission.

Gospel in a Puralist Society by Lesslie Newbigin © 2014 SPCK Classics. Reproduced with permission of the Licensor through PLSclear.

In our NEW Christian Doctrine Series

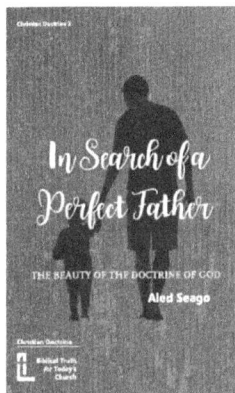

The most fundamental question in existence is this: who is God? The answer to this question will define everything concerning you, and the world you live in. God has revealed himself to us, and he reveals to us his utter perfection. That is beautiful.

This book is aimed to be a basic introduction to the doctrine of God, and particularly, the assurance his nature brings to us. Whether we have good or bad relationships with our fathers, seeing God as who he is: a perfect Father, is guaranteed to lift our souls beyond our limited, subjective circumstances. Let your soul sing as you discover, or are refreshed in, the perfection of our heavenly Father!

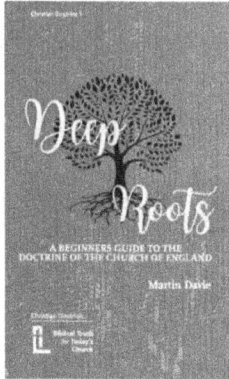

Those authorised to minister in the Church of England, whether as ordained or lay ministers, are expected to teach and act in accordance with the Church of England's doctrine. However, many of those who are currently exercising ministry in the Church of England, or who are being trained for ministry, are unclear about what the Church of England's doctrine is, and why it matters that they should adhere to it.

In order to address this situation, the Latimer Trust is producing a new series of short books on doctrine which are designed to introduce various key aspects of the doctrine of the Church of England. The purpose of *Deep Roots* is to introduce the series as a whole. It does this by explaining what doctrine is, the nature of the doctrinal authorities accepted by the Church of England, and why it is important for both ministers (and Christians in general) to adhere to what is taught by these doctrinal authorities.

This is a book for existing ministers, those in training for ministry and ordinary lay Christians who want a concise but reliable answer to the question 'What is doctrine and why does it matter?'

In our Christian Leadership series

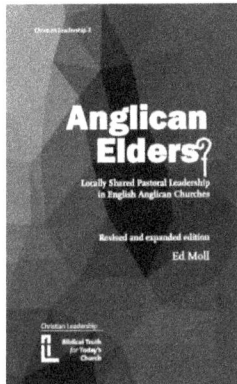

Anglican polity has traditionally favoured the incumbent as sole elder over a congregation. Biblical and missional imperatives press for eldership to be plural but how can this be done within an Anglican setting?

This study explores the biblical and historical background to plural eldership or locally shared pastoral leadership. It goes on to describe the experience of nine UK Anglican pastors who have established a team that functions as a plural eldership. While the focus is on the church's ministry of making disciples, lessons are drawn for other areas of pastoral leadership.

The revised and expanded edition includes additional chapters on the role of women and on the place of power in pastoral ministry.

A new Latimer Briefing

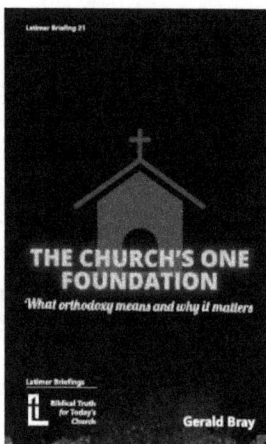

What is orthodoxy? In recent controversies in the Church of England and in the wider Anglican Communion, those who insist that the Church's traditional teachings about marriage and celibacy cannot be altered are increasingly described as 'orthodox', a claim that has been disputed on the ground that orthodoxy is defined by the great creeds and confessions of the Church, none of which mentions the subject.

This Briefing argues that orthodoxy extends well beyond what the creeds and confessions state. It is rooted in the mind of Christ, which is revealed to us in Holy Scripture and encompasses every aspect of life, including our doctrine and practice of matrimony. Orthodoxy is expressed not only in creeds but also in the forms of our worship, not least in the rich tradition of hymnody that has stood the test of time. Christians of every tradition resonate with orthodoxy because it bears witness to the presence of the Holy Spirit in our hearts, as he illuminates and applies the Word of God to our lives.

Using the words of the well-known hymn *The Church's One Foundation*, Gerald Bray demonstrates what orthodoxy is and why it matters both to individual believers and to the Church as a whole. In every generation we are challenged by new heresies and divisions that seek to lead us astray. Orthodoxy is the unchanging teaching of Christ given to us in the Bible as the resource we need to combat them. It unites us with the saints of the past, the present and the future in the spiritual warfare that engages God's people as we make our way to the heavenly kingdom promised to all true followers of Jesus.

www.ingramcontent.com/pod-product-compliance
Lightning Source LLC
La Vergne TN
LVHW041155080426
835511LV00006B/609